797,885 Books

are available to read at

Forgotten Books

www.ForgottenBooks.com

Forgotten Books' App
Available for mobile, tablet & eReader

ISBN 978-1-331-50481-8
PIBN 10199125

This book is a reproduction of an important historical work. Forgotten Books uses state-of-the-art technology to digitally reconstruct the work, preserving the original format whilst repairing imperfections present in the aged copy. In rare cases, an imperfection in the original, such as a blemish or missing page, may be replicated in our edition. We do, however, repair the vast majority of imperfections successfully; any imperfections that remain are intentionally left to preserve the state of such historical works.

Forgotten Books is a registered trademark of FB &c Ltd.
Copyright © 2015 FB &c Ltd.
FB &c Ltd, Dalton House, 60 Windsor Avenue, London, SW19 2RR.
Company number 08720141. Registered in England and Wales.

For support please visit www.forgottenbooks.com

1 MONTH OF FREE READING

at

www.ForgottenBooks.com

By purchasing this book you are eligible for one month membership to ForgottenBooks.com, giving you unlimited access to our entire collection of over 700,000 titles via our web site and mobile apps.

To claim your free month visit:

www.forgottenbooks.com/free199125

* Offer is valid for 45 days from date of purchase. Terms and conditions apply.

Similar Books Are Available from
www.forgottenbooks.com

Poems
by Edgar Allan Poe

The Complete Poetical Works and Letters of John Keats
by John Keats

Erotica
by Arthur Clark Kennedy

The Complete Poetical Works of John Milton
by John Milton

One Hundred Poems of Kabir
by Kabir

The Barons' Wars, Nymphidia, and Other Poems
by Michael Drayton

A Book of English Poetry
by George Beaumont

Poems: Sonnets, Lyrics, and Miscellaneous
by Edward Blackadder

The Book of Fairy Poetry
by Dora Owen

Chinese Poems
by Charles Budd

Coleridge's The Rime of the Ancient Mariner
And Other Poems, by Samuel Taylor Coleridge

Complaints; Containing Sundrie Small Poemes of the Worlds Vanitie
Whereof the Next Page Maketh Mention, by Edmund Spenser

The Complete Poetical Works of Geoffrey Chaucer
Now First Put Into Modern English, by John S. P. Tatlock

Cursor Mundi (The Cursor of the World)
A Northumbrian Poem of the XIVth Century, by Richard Morris

The Defence of the Bride Other Poems
by Anna Katharine Green

The Divine Comedy, Vol. 1
by Dante Alighieri

The Duke of Gandia
by Algernon Charles Swinburne

Eanthe
A Tale of the Druids, and Other Poems, by Sandford Earle

The Earthly Paradise
A Poem, by William Morris

The English Poems of George Herbert
Newly Arranged in Relation to His Life, by George Herbert Palmer

THE
𝔓oetical 𝔚orks
OF
JAMES CHAMBERS,

Itinerant Poet,

WITH THE LIFE OF THE AUTHOR.

From lowest place, when virtuous things proceed,
The place is dignified by the doer's deed.
For 'tis the mind that makes the body rich,
And, as the Sun breaks through the darkest clouds
So honor peereth in the meanest habit.
What, is the jay more precious than the lark,
Because his feathers are more beautiful?
Or is the adder better than the eel
Because his painted skin contents the eye.
No.————————————————

SHAKSPEARE.

Entered at Stationers' Hall.

IPSWICH:

PRINTED FOR AND SOLD BY THE EDITOR, C RAGAN,
SOLD ALSO BY COWELL, BUTTER-MARKET, AND ALL OTHER BOOKSELLERS.

1820.

UNIV. OF
CALIFORNIA

CONTENTS.

	Page
Life, &c.	iii
Acrostic on the Author's Name, the first he ever composed.	7
Acrostic on a Dismal Thunder Storm, *(Dear Sirs, the Author of this Poem took refuge in a House on Evans Heath, during that dismal Thunder Storm.)*	8
Verses on a Barn being burnt down in the above Thunder Storm.	13
The Author's Journey to Woodbridge after the Storm.	16
The Poor Phytologist, or the Author gathering herbs.	18
Lines on a Conference at a Funeral.	29

	Page
Morning Winter Piece.	38
Evening Winter Piece, first Part.	48
Evening Winter Piece, second Part.	55
The Wounded Soldier's Return.	60
Lines on a dismal Thunder Storm in winter time.	63
On the Death of Lord Nelson.	69
Lines on a Little Black Dog stealing the Author's Meat.	73
On a Brinded Greyhound carrying a piece of meat to the Author.	77
On a Maid Servant killing two Cats.	80
Anecdote on Sir Philip and his Goat, or a caution against Ebriety.	83
The Pig Hunt.	91
Lines on a Gift of Coals to the Poor by Lady Rowley, at Stoke by Nayland.	94
On the Opening of a New Peal of Eight Bells, the Gift of the Right Hon. the Earl of Dysart.	100
The Author's Second Day at Helmingham.	109
Noah's Ark.	114
Verses Written in Great Bealings Church-yard.	117

	Page
Lines made by the Author when a Little Boy, on a Journey with his Father to Wicken Hall.	122
On the Benevolence of a Friend.	125
Verses on Grundisburgh Fair.	128
The Poor Poetaster.	133
Verses on a Rat knawing Twine, and winding it many times round the Bed-post.	143
Serious Reflections on a Thunder Storm.	147
Acrostic, (William Moore, Plumber, Glazier, and Painter.	151
Double Acrostic, (William Damant, Clarissa Gross.)	154
Acrostic on the Author's Name.	156
Acrostic on Harvest, (James Chambers, Acrostic Maker.)	157
Double Acrostic, (John Pitcher, Woodbridge, Betsy Browne, Southwold.)	159
Double Acrostic, (Ann Prest, Lewisham, is a Courteous Lady.)	160
Double Acrostic, (Mr. Samuel Golden, a Waiter in a Shop.)	161

the same poetic turn of mind, as far as the hurry of business would admit of the indulgence of it. His first poem appears to have been an acrostic on his own name.—Numerous were the early productions in this style, which he has in his travels dispersed about the country, to the no small fame of a match and net-seller. Verses, then, (as now,) were composed by him without any premeditation, or very close attention, and the profits accruing from them, came often, opportunely, to satisfy the cravings of a half-fed stomach, which he has, through a series of 72 years, often experienced with sorrow. By thirst he is seldom distressed, a pool or brook containing that which he expresses great pleasure in drinking—nevertheless, meeting, at times, with a more substantial cordial, he is very thankful that home-brewed beer has the pre-eminence among those, who charitably slake his parched lungs, though he seldom gives that verbal thankfulness, which, on his part, politeness would make proper.—As to apparel (as in most other things pertaining to the external comfort of rational creatures) he discovers no taste, though an uncommon peculiarity; any thread-bare worn cast-off vestment wants no fashionable criterion to recommend it to his service, so that a more wretched appearance and combination of rags and filth, words are not capable of describing—his visage nearly excluded from the public eye, by the uncouth manner of wearing a tattered hat, his feet exposed to the rough greetings of stones, gravel, and wet, and his whole frame, at times, to the rude blasts and gelid visits of the wintry storm.—From what he has been induced to perform, at any time the greatest confidence may be reposed in him. Truth, honesty, and every ingredient requisite to the composition of an upright mind, he certainly possesses. —Cruelty (a stain upon rationality) he holds in detestation, and was never known to commit any action that could be justly challenged as such.

He himself avers that his only attendance at school was for the space of a month in his childhood, which, from a happy strong recollection he remembers; this assertion gave rise to the following lines:—

> This man, on whom a Poet's gift is pour'd,
> With proper cultivation, might have tow'rd
> Beyond Parnassus Mount, of worth sublime
> Transcended every effort made in rhyme.—
> Brought to perfection every latent spark
> Of erudition—and with wing of lark—
> Soar'd o'er all former bounds, with strength intense
> Explor'd each nook of learning, in the expanse—

the same poetic turn of mind, as far as the hurry of business would admit of the indulgence of it. His first poem appears to have been an acrostic on his own name.—Numerous were the early productions in this style, which he has in his travels dispersed about the country, to the no small fame of a match and net-seller. Verses, then, (as now,) were composed by him without any premeditation, or very close attention, and the profits accruing from them, came often, opportunely, to satisfy the cravings of a half-fed stomach, which he has, through a series of 72 years, often experienced with sorrow. By thirst he is seldom distressed, a pool or brook containing that which he expresses great pleasure in drinking—nevertheless, meeting, at times, with a more substantial cordial, he is very thankful that home-brewed beer has the pre-eminence among those, who charitably slake his parched lungs, though he seldom gives that verbal thankfulness, which, on his part, politeness would make proper.—As to apparel (as in most other things pertaining to the external comfort of rational creatures) he discovers no taste, though an uncommon peculiarity; any thread-bare worn cast-off vestment wants no fashionable criterion to recommend it to his service, so that a more wretched appearance and combination of rags and filth, words are not capable of describing—his visage nearly excluded from the public eye, by the uncouth manner of wearing a tattered hat, his feet exposed to the rough greetings of stones, gravel, and wet, and his whole frame, at times, to the rude blasts and gelid visits of the wintry storm.—From what he has been induced to perform, at any time the greatest confidence may be reposed in him. Truth, honesty, and every ingredient requisite to the composition of an upright mind, he certainly possesses. —Cruelty (a stain upon rationality) he holds in detestation, and was never known to commit any action that could be justly challenged as such.

He himself avers that his only attendance at school was for the space of a month in his childhood, which, from a happy strong recollection he remembers; this assertion gave rise to the following lines :—

> This man, on whom a Poet's gift is pour'd,
> With proper cultivation, might have tow'rd
> Beyond Parnassus Mount, of worth sublime
> Transcended every effort made in rhyme.—
> Brought to perfection every latent spark
> Of erudition—and with wing of lark—
> Soar'd o'er all former bounds, with strength intense
> Explor'd each nook of learning, in the expanse—

With vig'rous intellect had shown the world
The muse's beauties like a sail unfurl'd—
But to thé fertile soil no tutor's care
Was e'er apply'd, the tender germ to rear!
Which of itself was thriving, and forbode
A plant extensive, admirably good.—

Nevertheless, from a self-cultivated mind, he is master of so much learning that it is wonderful, considering it is the result of untutor'd genius, and cannot fail to draw forth due praise and admiration.—It is scarcely justifiable to give him the appellation of Linguist, though he has a smattering of several languages.

Perhaps it may be proper to mention that in the course of his life he has been obliged to submit himself to Soham Workhouse; the reader may judge of his sentiments on that subject from a Poem entitled the "Poor Poetaster," and also from an account given of him by Mr. Webb, in the *Suffolk Garland*, which will be inserted in its place.—Leaving this abode, so repugnant to his feelings, he again became the wandering object already described, having, for the most part when travelling, no other lodging than what a barn, stable, pigstye, or the field has offered to him, wanting the means to procure any accommodation suitable to a weary traveller, and discovering such wretchedness as to induce the generality of people to reject him as a lodger. The Author was never christened, or married, though he formerly made some progression towards matrimony, by forming an acquaintance with a young woman, who, after a number of unsuccessful solicitations and hapless endeavours, left him a prey to the pungent pangs of disappointment. His residence, at this time, is at Woodbridge, in a hut near where the barracks formerly stood, in a condition extremely squalid, and unable, from its decayed state, to screen him from the chilling intrusion of inclement air; yet, there it is he sometimes reclines during the night, (surrounded by the impure stench of the interior, and a mass of filth which forms a mound at the door,) on a couch of dried herbs, where, if the invasion of its numerous inmates of terror (which prohibit him from sleeping) were excluded, he would prefer his homely gear and solitary abode to the pomp and splendour of a more eligible sphere. But alas! though he may call it his bed, it is far from administering to his jaded spirits

"Tir'd nature's sweet restorer balmy sleep."

He is constantly attended with a company of dogs, formerly four or more in number, but from an inability to procure sustenance for those mute followers of his misery, he has been obliged to retrench, and has only two left.

The following account of the Author is given in the *Suffolk Garland:*—

"His general appearance is wretched in the extreme; for many years he has wandered about different villages, subsisting on the charity of the inhabitants, and such passengers as are moved to pity by his forlorn and miserable appearance; he constantly ranges about in all weathers, from morning to night, and seems insensible of the worst—in this wretched manner does he subsist, always sleeping in the fields, an outhouse, or under some hedge, wherever night happens to overtake him; he is always attended by a large company of dogs, who share his scanty pittance, and who watch over his repose. Utterly averse to every degree of restraint and confinement, the thought of a poor-house, that place where—

"In one house throughout their lives to be
The pauper palace which they hate to see,
That giant building, that high-bounding wall,
Those bare-worn walks, that lofty thundering hall,
That large loud clock which tells each dreaded hour,
Those gates and locks, and all those signs of power,
It is a prison with a milder name
Which few inhabit without dread or shame—"

is almost death to him, and the horror of being confined to such a revolting abode, which continually haunts his mind, he pathetically describes in his Poem, entitled "The Poor Poetaster."

In 1810, Mr. Cordy, of Worlingworth, very kindly and humanely interested himself in behalf of the poor itinerant Poet, and published a statement of his case in the Ipswich Journal as follows :—

Sir,—A friend of mine has lately published a volume of Poems, in one of which entitled "Haverhill," are the following lines and note subjoined :—

>Near yonder bridge, that strides the ripling brook,
>A hut once stood, in small sequester'd nook,
>Where Chambers* lodg'd: though not of gipsy race,
>Yet, like that tribe, he often chang'd his place.
>A lonely wand'rer he, whose squalid form
>Bore the rude peltings of the wintry storm:
>An hapless outcast, on whose natal day
>No star propitious beam'd a kindly ray;
>By some malignant influence doom'd to roam
>The world's wide, dreary waste, and know no home.
>Yet heaven, to cheer him as he pass'd along,

---

* James Chambers, an itinerant Poet, travelled the country selling books, and occasionally, some of his own printed compositions; he could read well, and has read much, but could

Infus'd in life's sour cup the sweets of song.
Oft on his couch of straw, or bed of hay,
This wand'ring poet tun'd th' *acrostic lay;*
On him the gentle muse her favours shed,
And nightly musings earn'd his daily bread.
Meek, unassuming, modest shade! forgive
This mean attempt to make thy mem'ry live;
To me more pleasing thus thy deeds to tell,
Than the proud task to sing how heroes fell.
Minstrel, adieu! to me thy fate's unknown;
Since last I saw thee many a year has flown:
Full oft has summer pour'd her fervid beams,
And winter's icy breath congeal'd the streams.

---

not write.* Sometimes he descended so low as to be a seller of matches. He gained no inconsiderable degree of celebrity by composing acrostics during the night, as he lay in a barn, hay-loft, or shed, and would procure some kind friend to be his amanuensis next day, † for which performances he sometimes received a crown, half-crown, or sixpence, and frequently in lieu of money, a meal.—He was a person of mild, unassuming, and inoffensive manners, and possessed a mind strongly tinctured with a sense of religion; he left Haverhill about 20 years since, and never returned afterwards.

* The author has acquired, I suppose, since then, a slight knowledge of the art.

† The following information I received from this eccentric character about three weeks since—" While I resided at Haverhill" said he " Mr. Webb, (the author of the Elegy on my Death) was my chief amanuensis; and he frequently said, while with me, that he wished he could learn to make Poetry; which art he has since accomplished." This seems to have been about 32 years ago. EDITOR, 6th June, 1820.

Perhaps, lorn wretch! unfriended and alone,
In hovel vile thou gav'st thy final groan;
Clos'd the blear eye, ordain'd no more to weep,
And sunk, unheeded sunk, in death's long sleep!
O how unlike the bard in higher sphere,
Whose fortunate numbers reach the polish'd ear;
Whose muse in academic bowers reclines,
And, cheer'd by affluence, pours her classic lines;
Whose sapient brow, though angry critics frown,
Boasts the green chaplet, and the laurel crown!

The subject of these remarks has been travelling from the age of 16 to his present age (62), in the same singular and abject condition, and is now in the neighbourhood of Earl Soham, in this county.—My only motive and sole object for troubling you on this occasion is—that, should casuality or sickness overtake this forlorn being, I sincerely hope and trust, that wherever it occurs, those around will take pity and compassion on the suffering wanderer, and not let one of the great family of mankind be neglected at such a period.—I feel, however, confident, that were it not for the too frequent impositions of the impudent and sturdy mendicant, few minds there are, in this liberal and enlightened age, who would not take compassion on this inoffensive object in distress. I knew little of this poor creature till my attention and curiosity were aroused, by hearing he was in this neighbourhood, and having the Poem of Haverhill come into my hands nearly at the same time, I brought him to my house, and found him to be a character greatly deserving of attention. It is astonishing to witness such capabilities of mind under the garb of extreme wretchedness. He was literally without clothing, and altogether in a state calculated to excite our sympathy, and the best feelings of the humane mind. He has written many hundred pieces of fugitive poetry, chiefly acrostics; and from this employment he seems to have procured his poor subsistence.— Incredible as it may appear, this poor itinerant composed an heroic poem on the death of Lord Nelson, which would have done credit to any book of poems ever published;—and far, very far, superior to most compositions of its kind abounding in sublime imagery, metaphor, and sentiment, equal to any poem (without exception) I ever read; and were it not for the idea that making the copy of that poem, and others he has composed public, might injure the sale of any collection he (through some kind friend) should get a subscription for, or get printed for sale, I should certainly give the words in your paper, and I have no doubt but the generality of your readers would be much gratified, and astonished that such compositions could originate from such a quarter.

This induced the late Duchess of Chandos, Countess of Dysart, Lord Henniker, &c. to send donations to him for the use of this solitary wanderer. A plan was accordingly formed to make him stationary, but an attempt might as well have been made to hedge in the cuckoo,—a cottage was hired at Worlingworth, and furnished, and his poems were to have been printed for his benefit, but alas! a scene of humble comfort seemed neither grateful to his mind, nor auspicious to his muse, for after residing there a month or two, he set off on one of his peregrinations, and returned no more; custom, doubtless, had wrought such a habit in his nature, that he really would have preferred the solitude of a sordid shed to the splendid enjoyments of a palace, and a bed of straw to a couch of down.

In the year 1818 he resided at Framlingham, in a miserable shed, at the back of the town, and daily walked to Earl Soham, or some of the neighbouring villages; his next route was for Woodbridge, which I believe has been his chief abode since that time.

Should any person be inclined to look contemptuously on these productions, arising from the abject state of the author, I wish them to read with attention the following remarks which are extracted from Bloomfield's ' Farmer's Boy,' and if it should be suspected that I insert them with any other view than for the reader to judge candidly, and not " despise the short and simple annals of the poor," they will do me great injustice :—

"It cannot be forgotten by any one who has thought of my history and success, that Mr. Lofft has said, when speaking of the M. S. of this Poem, that it had before been shown to some persons in London, whose indifference towards it may probably be explained, when it is considered, that it came to their hands under no circumstances of adventitious recommendation.—With some, a person must be rich, or titled, or fashionable, as a literary name, or at least fashionable in some respect, good or bad, before any thing which he can offer will be thought worthy of notice. Nothing surely can so effectually illustrate this fact as a plain account of my unsuccessful attempts, in publicly stating which, on uch an occasion as this, I see not the smallest impropriety, as it may teach men in my own station of life not to despair, if they feel themselves morally and intellectually worthy of notice; and, at the same time, teach them not to rely on an untried and brittle support, by throwing away the honorable staff of mechanic independence.—After stating the facts, and explaining the ill-treatment (as it must be termed) he received, on offering the M. S. of his Poem, he thus concludes :—

" I have the gratification to know that this Poem has given, pleasure to thousands, and to make a contrary pretence would be something worse than affectation. Upon conviction I rest my claim (with all due submission to the learned) of exhorting all persons of acknowledged taste and ability, when they receive a poor man's production; to read it with candour, and to judge of it with truth, so that if it be found entitled to a share of public attention, the unlettered and the unfriended may not lose their chance of communicating instruction or entertainment to the world."

TO THE READER.

Many, probably, on hearing the character and appearance of the Author of these Poems, may prepossess themselves very unfavourably as to the worth of them. But as prejudice (as many of his readers will doubtless allow from experience) is often erroneous, and reversed, after an accurate examination, it is earnestly hoped, and sanguinely anticipated, that it will, after a perusal, meet with a defeat, however obdurately it may be implanted in the mind, when candour, with deliberate and unbiassed feelings advances, and foil the abrupt conceptions originating in an unreasonable and ungrounded opinion.

The author truly lives in a despicable state of wretchedness, apparrelled in the most unsightly, and filthy rags; but as the addition of fine splendid robes conveys no refinement of sentiment to the wearer, neither can the tattered weeds of indigence smother, enervate, or contract the genuine vigor of poetic effusion, emanating from real genius.

We mean no disparagement to virtuous wealth, but poverty is by no means degenerating or lessening to the mind of the owner.

Pigmies are pigmies still, tho' perch'd on Alps,
And pyramids are pyramids in vales.
Each man makes his own stature. Virtue alone
Outbuilds the pyramids, her monuments shall last
When Egypts fall. YOUNG.

Since then the garb cannot delineate the mind, affluence add, nor indigence diminish, (when combined with content,) the sterling flowings of the heart, impartiality, prompted by humanity, will admit of no such obstacles to a circumstanced candid decision.

Since then the garb cannot delineate the mind, affluence add, nor indigence diminish, (when combined with content,) the sterling flowings of the heart, impartiality, prompted by humanity, will admit of no such obstacles to a stream, clogged canuid designs.

As the insertion of the whole of the Subscribers names to the following work would be enlarging it to no purpose, the editor hopes, that those who are omitted will not impute it to any disrepect or ingratitude; he contents himself with inserting those who have in the greatest degree befriended the author.

THE EARL OF ROCHFORD, 2 copies.
J. COBBOLD, ESQ. Holywells
J. READ, ESQ 3 copies.
COUNT LINSENGEN, 2 copies.
MRS. TROTMAN, 2 copies.
MRS. KERRIDGE, Whitton

ERRATA.

Page	Line			
14	13	for	resplendid read	resplendent
20	18		diarrhœtic	diuretick
34	9		revenge was join'd	reverie join'd,
42	12		insur'd	insued
48	1		In winter time	In the winter time
64	7		For to	For so to
77	8		Brinded	Brindled
109	1		Wednesday	Tuesday
109	2		seem'd	seems
117	5		tomb	stone
142	7		some mansions	Soham mansions

POEMS.

Acrostic

ON THE AUTHOR'S NAME,

THE FIRST HE EVER COMPOSED.

J ames Chambers is my name,

A nd I am scorn'd by rich and poor,

M any a weary step I came,

E nduring hardships very sore;

S o I design to take a wife,

C an I but have one to my mind,

H enceforth to live a better life,

A nd then we may true solace find;

M ay I but have the lass I love,

B oth to each other constant prove,

E ndeavour thus to live in peace,

R enewing love in every case,

S o to remain till life does cease.

Acrostic

ON A DISMAL THUNDER STORM.

(The Initials form the words) *Dear Sirs, the Author of this Poem took refuge in a House on Evans-Heath, during that dismal Thunder Storm.*

D readful one Thursday ev'ning 'twas indeed,

(E re death arrests may we repent with speed,)

A t Halstead and near to Stowmarket town,

R ipe corn and hay consum'd, and barns burnt down;

S urely my friends a dire nocturnal scene,

I n which such dreary clouds did intervene,

R efulgent lightnings flash and thunders roll,
S bould each excite to mind his precious soul.
T he afternoon preceding that dread night,
H ow did the rising storm my mind affright;
E ach gloomy prospect 'chas'd away delight;
A doleful sound address'd my listening ear,
U nceasing thunder I at distance hear;
T he place called Hadleigh-Heath I travers'd o'er,
H ow fearless till I heard the thunder roar;
O solemn thought, what danger imminent,
R eplete with horror did the scene present,
O 'er all the sable vesture seems to spread,
Fears still increas'd,—my heart was fill'd with dread;
T wo fields I walk'd, a cottage did espy,
H ere I took shelter, while the storm drew nigh ;
I, with domestics of the rustic train,
S uch favours found as somewhat sooth'd my pain,

Put all your trust said they now in the Lord,
Obey his voice and tremble at his word!
Ere long the thunder with its awful sound,
More fierce and more the cottage did surround,
Tremendous lightning with a lustre bright,
O'er woods and fields illum'd the darksome night;
O, what a dreary scene, no neighbour nigh,—
Kind heaven defend and spare us or we die,
Repeated peals of thunder still resound,
Effulgent flashes rapid blazed around.
Fear came on all, for conscience all accus'd,
Unfelt before, though oft before abus'd,
Guilty and vile, aloud did seem to cry,
Entirely lost, poor wretch, where wilt thou fly?
In ev'ry place this monitor within,
Notices all our ways, rebukes for sin,
A faithful witness does the thoughts descry,
How oft I've it abus'd, alas thought I!

O should the inclement lightning strike me dead,
U nited sheets of sulphurous flames my bed
S urely must deck, where I must justly bear
E ternal torments, horrors, and despair;
O may we ne'er see that infernal place,
N o solace there, no glimmering rays of grace;—
E ternity! I tremble at the word,
V enture yourselves, my friends, upon the Lord,
A lenient balm he has to heal our smart,
N ought but his love can melt th' obdurate heart;
S eek fervently in time his free rich grace,
H is love implore, his righteousness and peace;
E mbrace my friends the glorious gospel plan,
A Saviour came to rescue sinful man,
T he bless'd Redeemer who from sin was free,
H as died to save vile wretches such as we,
D elight in him ye saints, admire his pow'r,
U nite to praise, in every trying hour,

B. 5

R evere heaven's sov'reignty and yet rejoice,
I ncline your ear to this majestic voice,
N o more may guilty fears the mind molest,
G race when prevailing cheers the languid breast,
'T is time to seek for mercy and repent,
H eaven's threat'ning voice may make hard hearts relent
A gift some have received, and it misus'd,
T alents some had, but greatly them abus'd,
D readful's the great supreme Almighty power,
I ndeed we are but creatures of an hour,
S oon can he crush a num'rous throng to dust,
M y soul adore his power,—in Jesus trust.
A las! one potent word might strike us dead,
L ifeless and cold t'embrace our pulverous bed.
T he lucid flashes how they strike the eye!
H ark! how loud bursts of thunder rend the sky,
U nusual scene, yet why thus droops my heart?
N one can us harm but sin's delusive art.

D read sov'reign take, these gloomy fears away,

E nlighten us with an all-cheering ray,

R everse the scene and change the night to day;

S hould storms of seven-fold thunder then arise,

T ear the strong pillows of the vaulted skies,

O r from its centre should this earth remove,

R enew'd by grace and heirs of endless love,

M ercy shall us await in brilliant realms above.

VERSES ON A

BARN BEING BURNT DOWN

IN THE ABOVE THUNDER STORM.

Celestial muse assist, my pen inspire,
   May rev'rence deep possess my thoughtful breast,
Replete with zeal and true poetic fire,
   May every sentiment be well express'd.

I'd chant the wonders of that power supreme,

    Who fram'd the earth and spread the starry sky,

That power by which, lost sinners to redeem,

    Emanuel came, and even deign'd to die.

Th' eternal deity great power exerts,

    In saving souls from the devouring lake,

And O what horrors seize poor trembling hearts,

    When from on high it does in thunder speak.

The ninth of August! O tremendous thought!

    What words the horrors of that night can paint?

Such wonders by that mighty power were wrought,

    As almost caus'd the stoutest heart to faint.

The lucid flashes with resplendid blaze,

    Loud sounds succeeding, shone o'er Halstead town,

Which struck the mind with tremor and amaze,

    While vivid fire with rapid speed came down;

With such velocity it did descend,
 It seized a new built barn with hay well stor'd,
Neighbours alarm'd soon came to assist their friend,
 But left the event to the all-powerful Lord.

A dreadful conflagration t'was indeed,
 Th' dismal sight a numerous concourse view'd,
Who with much work and engines did proceed,
 Till they at length the raging fire subdu'd.

The worthy master of the inn we hear,
 To whom the barn and premises belong'd,
Supplied his well-proved friends with liquors clear,
 While gazing multitudes around him throng'd.

The Author though at Evans-Heath that night,
 Had thoughts some days revolving in his breast,
To walk to Halstead at the dawn of light,
 And in that barn his usual place to rest;

Yet had he slept there, one supreme command
  Could cause the fervid flames to lose their pow'r,
He who saved others by his mighty hand,
  Could him preserve in that tremendous hour.

THE AUTHOR'S
JOURNEY TO WOODBRIDGE
AFTER THE STORM.

The worthless author of these simple rhymes
  T'is true, was once in a superior state,
But losses, crosses, and these trying times,
  Had lately him reduc'd to sufferings great.

In April, he from Ipswich did retire,
  O'er verdant meads, in much distress of mind,
Woodbridge to see was his intense desire,
  Firmly believing he should friendship find;

Replete with keen remorse and discontent,
   Quite penny-less 'mongst men superb he stray'd,
Contemptuous smiles from cynicks did resent,
   Yet did not quite distrust celestial aid.

At length some gentlemen beneficent,
   Excited by rich grace and love divine,
To sooth his fears and give his mind content,
   To raise a small subscription did incline,

That these plain verses might in print appear,
   Which he on that dread thunder storm compos'd;
ay all who read them serve their God with fear,
   Ere by death's chilling hand their eyes are clos'd.

THE
Poor Phytologist,
OR THE AUTHOR GATHERING HERBS.

When bright Aurora gilds the eastern skies,
I wake, and from my squalid couch arise;
Brisk Philomela tunes her dulcet lay,
The lark arising, hails the op'ning day,
The plumed choirs with cheerful accents rise,
And chant their matins to th' etherial skies,
The whole creation seems combin'd to raise
A sacred anthem to celestial praise.
I rise invested with my tatter'd dress,
Grateful sensations could to heaven express;
(Was I enrob'd with ornaments divine,
Garments that all superb attire outshine:)

My clothes in sleeping hours my covering were
From chilling blasts, and from the inclement air,
These screen'd me from the cold in some degree,
Yet much I felt—the light I gladly see;
But why should I distrust, or e'er repine?
Let me my will to providence resign,
The Saviour slumber'd in as mean a bed,
He'd scarce a place to rest his sacred head:
I suffer much, perhaps for some good end,
To sooth my fears, kind heaven may raise a friend,
I'll bless his name who has my frame upheld,
Then walk the mead and dew bespangled field;
Bright Phœbus rising, darts a cheering beam,
Awakes the muse, I choose some fav'rite theme,
Urania fair my fainting mind inspire,
And warm my languid mind with sacred fire,
Be this my topic, this my aim and end,
Heaven's will t'obey, and seek t'oblige a friend.

c

I walk'd in vernal hours o'er meadows gay,

And view'd bright florid scenes in smiling May;

Pastures o'erspread with Cowslips we behold,

Illum'd by solar rays like glist'ning gold;

These flowers are of narcotic parts possest,

They sooth to sleep, and give the patient rest;

I pluck them while bright Sol does fulgid shine,

Then dry them to procure heart-cheering wine.

Some herbs adorn the hills—some vales below

Where limpid streamlets in meanders flow,

Here's golden Saxifrage, in vernal hours,

Springs up when water'd well by fertile showers,

It flourishes in bogs where waters beat,

The yellow flowers in clusters stand complete,

Adorn'd with snowy white in meadows low,

White Saxifrage displays a lucid show,

The roots, or seeds a special powder make,

Which friends may as a diarrhœtic take;

Gromwell's fair vestment decks the purling rill,

Parsley-Break-Stone adorns the rising hill,

With these good herbs some service might be done

With ease, t' expel the gravel and the stone;

Here's Golden Rod too for this purpose sent,

These pungent keen sensations to prevent;

Why should my friends in pining grief remain,

Or suffer with excruciating pain?

These wholesome med'cines, if by heaven blest,

Sure anodynes will prove, and give them rest;

Bright Sol ascending, splendid light displays,

Revives the landscape with meridian rays,

The dews dispel'd, all nature now looks gay,

Th' enamel'd meads expand their bright array;

As fervid sultry rays the air pervade,

I leave the fields, and walk the sylvan shade,

In this retreat I taste the vernal breeze,

Explore the verdant plants and 'tow'ring trees,

Reject each baneful herb and choose the good,
Such as are fit for med'cine, or for food ;
Some herbs I in the fields and meads have found,
I safe reserve to heal a neighbour's wound ;
Within this grove some sanent herbs I view,
Health to preserve and cure the wounded too.
Here's Tormentilla, with its searching parts,
Expels the pois'nous venom from our hearts,
By perspiration 'twill the cure effect ;
In needful seasons ne'er this herb neglect,
An emblem this of hearts defiled with sin,
And his rich love who makes them pure and clean,
Who once perspir'd with agonizing pain,
To cleanse our hearts from every guilty stain ;
Come guilty sin-sick patients as you are,
Nor e'er reject the kind physician's care,
He knows your griefs and pains, and will impart
Reviving cordials to each languid heart.

Woodbetony is in its prime in May,
In June and July does its bloom display,.
A fine bright red does this grand plant adorn,
To gather it for drink I think no scorn,
I'll make a conserve of its fragrant flow'rs,
Its spicy flavour in cold gelid hours.
Will help the stomach when we loath our meat,
And will a pleasing appetite create;
Cephalick virtues in this herb remain,
To chace each dire disorder from the brain,
Delirious persons here a cure may find,
To stem the phrensy, and to calm the mind,
All authors own Woodbetony is good,
'Tis king o'er all the herbs that deck the wood;
A king's physician erst such notice took.
Of this, he on its virtues wrote a book;
But now by toil and fervid heat deprest,
Beneath the spreading oak awhile I rest,

Here I reflect on that supernal power,

Whose pencil ting'd each variegated flower,

No less than the Supreme, o'er heaven and earth,

Whose fiat gave this gay creation birth;

To read his sacred word I now incline,

And wish to view rich grace in every line,

Select some passages, the book I close,

Then take my pen a poem to compose;

To Neighbours thus I'll friendly caution give,

Who knows but some may real good receive?

To find more herbs to do the afflicted good,

I leave the groves to range the extensive wood,

The first choice herb presented to my view,

Is Sanicula in its blooming hue,

With snow white flowers a precious herb indeed,

To heal intrinsic ails in time of need;

With other herbs, it cures external wounds,

The fame of this in every place resounds;

I'll plant it in my garden, there 'twill grow,
That many friends its real worth may know :
Ranging the trackless vales, at length I find,
An herb long sought with an attentive mind,
Herb Paris 'tis, the stem is long and small,
The vulgar this rare plant herb True-love call;
A curious plant, by authors known full well,
With other herbs all poison to expel;
So, by experience, we may sometimes find,
True love expels the poison of the mind;
True love expands the heart to ev'ry friend,
But most to real christians 'twill extend.
The sun descends towards the western skies,
Dense clouds to obscure the atmosphere arise,
Rapid I to my rural cot repair,
My vestment scarce defends from chilling air,
My languid heart for some refreshment pants,—
But first I'll set my curious herbs and plants,

These may compensate all my toilsome hours,
If water'd soon by fertilizing showers,
I, in my garden little room bestow
At present, for herbaceous plants to grow,
'Tis with potatoes now almost replete,
So that the herbs and they together meet;
Two lovely fruit-trees and a spreading vine,
Adorn my garden—why should I repine?
In freezing months, if life and health remain,
Potatoes may my feeble frame sustain,
And should I have success with my small vine,
My drooping heart will be refresh'd with wine;
But I may leave them, ere the setting sun,
If called hence—the Almighty's will be done!
I enter now my mean repast to take,
And if I'm one who suffers for Christ's sake,
Though void of furniture my food to dress,
Yet he'll the meanest morsel deign to bless:

Should I enabled be, utensils buy,
Some wholesome food I'd often boil or fry,
A friend with me on richest herbs might dine,
In mutual peace, and drink domestic wine,
Enjoying mind serene, and true content,
Well pleas'd with what kind heaven in mercy sent;
If with the Saviour's gracious presence blest,
Our hearts are cheer'd by so divine a guest,
More real solace 'twill the mind afford,
Than all the dainties of the festal board;
No more I'll envy those, whose sumptuous fare
And luscious juices, oft become a snare,
Who Ophir's gold and Tyrian purple wear;
Be calm my mind, subside ye trying times,
And soar my muse beyond these sordid climes,
Behold a table richly spread on high,
In blissful mansions 'bove the expansive sky,
Where rich and poor in peaceful union meet,
There saints are in their glorious head complete,

With joy they on delicious viands feast,

While recent wine supplies the rich repast,

There grand parterres and lovely gardens view,

And florets blooming in most beauteous hue,

There limpid streams of pleasure ever glide,

This scene transcends terrestrial pomp and pride.

Ah! blissful state where foes no more distress,

No haughty tyrants humble saints oppress,

All partial pride for ever done away,

Pure love shines perfect as meridian day;

Kind heaven' suppress by faith all anxious fears,

Give true content in this dark vale of tears:

Surmounting ev'ry trial on the road,

May I ascend to that sublime abode,

Gladly I'd leave all sublunary joy,

And fading scenes which might true peace destroy,

To join the favor'd throng in tuneful strains,

And sing free grace and love through blissful plains.

LINES ON A

CONFERENCE AT A FUNERAL.

One afternoon I walk'd the sylvan shade,

While solar rays illum'd the sultry glade,

In the serene reviving month of June,

Wing'd songsters chanted with melodious tune,

Bright fields with florid verdure were array'd,

And vernal scenes most beauteously display'd;

To muse near trickling rills, or roseate bow'rs,

Or crop rich foilage 'mid th' expanding flow'rs,

Descending eastern hills, I walk'd the street,

Where beau and peasant miscellaneous meet,

Near ev'ry portal, ev'ry entrance gate,

Ladies and gentlemen complaisant wait,

To see a solemn funeral display'd;
Some seem alert, and others much dismay'd:
Ere long dense clouds gloom all the azure skies,
Loud bursts of thunder timid minds surprise;
The lofty church reflects the awful sound,
While vivid flashes lucid blaz'd around,
The tempest hush'd, what gazing crouds did meet,
To see the mourning train pervade the street,
To view those lovely nymphs, in bloom of years,
(Miss V. precedes,) there all suffus'd in tears:
Rayment of sable hue does some invest,
Others like bride-maids in white robes were dress'd,
Those black as ravens' plumes attract the eye,
These with the milk-white snow-drop well may vie;
Their mild address, their graceful air and mien,
Conspire to decorate the dirgic scene,
The dear remains six sturdy yeomen bear,
Lovers and friends of the deceased fair,

These all her polish'd beauties once admir'd,
Who now in sable vestment are attir'd.
A stranger treads the consecrated ground,
While transient views his curious mind astound;
He audience gives, yea, all atttenive hear
The funeral rites perform'd with rev'rend fear,
While fervent pray'r t' etherial realms aspires,
The cause of pungent woe he thus enquires:
A solemn scene, alas! Sirs, does appear,
What means the rising sigh, the gushing tear?
Why pearly drops bedew the mourner's eye,
And sullen gloom o'erwhelm the stander-by?
Has some respectful yeoman lost his bride,
Crop'd like a flower in all its gaudy pride?
Or has the am'rous suitor lost his love?
Comforts terrene grim death does oft remove;
The lifeless mass to pulv'rous earth must turn,
Why weep those plaintive virgins o'er her urn?

O ! cries a friend, I tremble to relate

How direful was this brisk young lady's fate,

Her coffin view, she's snatch'd from life's gay stage,

Dated no more than seventeen years of age;

A kindred swain, enamour'd with her charms,

Indulg'd a wish to take her to his arms,

He near two years express'd his ardent love,

But often griev'd lest she should faithless prove;

A dancing ball adorn'd our recent fair,

Gay beaux and belles alert assembled there,

The am'rous swain, 'tis said, a rival found,

Which him induc'd the tender fair to wound:

Suspicion dire his vengeful bosom warm'd,

Next morn the horrid business was perform'd;

I fear he did premeditate the strife,

Some weeks ere this he bought a pocket-knife,

Lest that should fail, as her dear life he sought,

He at Saint George's Fair a hog-knife bought

With this he boldly enters in the morn,

Ere bright Aurora orient hills adorn:

Sure the assassin had no good design—

The lady on her sofa did recline;

He ask'd her if she did him truly love—

She said she'd as a friend of him approve;

He ask'd a kind salute, she'd not comply,

Virtue and modesty must this deny;

Some think he in a phrenzy seiz'd the knife,

Depriv'd the lady of her precious life;

Sure he must act the inflated tyrant's part,

Who stabs the much-lov'd object to the heart;

Re-pierc'd by cruel steel she suffer'd pain,

While sanguine gore perven'd each thrilling vein,

But as none saw him do the stygian deed,

'Tis thought he'll be from penal suff'rings freed.

Eight hours she liv'd, did all the truth declare,

In agony expir'd the blooming fair.

As characters unsullied both sustain'd,
Each heart susceptible of grief is pain'd,
His courteous conduct gave some friends delight
Her reputation shone with lustre bright.
If truth appears in what the vulgar say,
What could induce the man his niece to slay?
We may, I think, his sentiments express,
'Twas that no other might her charms caress;
Illusion sure, with dire revenge was join'd,
His frame enerv'd, inflam'd his am'rous mind,
Or baleful influence, from pale Cynthia's wane,
Had render'd all his mental powers insane;
Bury Assizes shortly will commence,
Some gentlemen will stand in his defence,
They'll plead his cause as one insane indeed,
Thus from a shameful exit he'll be freed;
Now since he's been in prison walls confin'd,
What doleful horrors seiz'd his gloomy mind,

His keen remorse, his pensive studious heart,
Give hope kind heaven will saving grace impart;
Should he be brought to punishment condign,
May courteous gentry, rev'rend and benign,
Who oft to visit his drear cell incline,
Through grace divine him to repentance bring,
That he may yet of sov'reign mercy sing!
But ah! why did the grizly monarch come
To crop the flower ere it was full in bloom;
The fairest flower that decks the od'rous vale,
Once fann'd by zephyr's breeze, or orient gale,
If Boreal blasts, or solar rays pervade,
Its bloom declines, its splendid beauties fade:
My friend, had you but seen this lovely fair
Pervade the verdant mead with sprightly air,
Or view'd those glist'ning orbs with brilliance shine,
Her lover priz'd her as a form divine;

What glowing blushes did those cheeks disclose,

Of vermil hue, which far outvied the rose;

But ah! how soon did that bright form decline,

The loveliest fair one must her breath resign;

Those rolling sparklers death's chill hand must close,

In silent gloom, to take a long repose,

At heaven's grand audit may she wake and rise

To blissful mansions, 'bove the expansive skies!

What cause for fruitless sorrow does appear?

Let dawning hope elude all anxious fear:

Whate'er transpires though we kind heav'n provoke

Mercy still blends with each bereaving stroke:

But ah! the social friend, the parent dear,

Can scarce restrain the sympathizing tear;

Oh! cruel lover, rigid is thy fate,

With tremor I the doleful tale relate;

No more, resumes the stranger, 'twill surprise,

If limpid torrents flow from languid eye

Sure 'twill to youth a timely warning prove,
To stem the risings of inord'nate love:
O may surviving friends their grief suppress,
May peace and hope celestial, give redress,
May ev'ry mourning friend true solace find,
Supernal love revive the drooping mind;
A competent narration thus I've gave,
Of friends conversing near a lady's grave,
Kind friends solicit me oft to rehearse
The tragic scene disclos'd in dirgic verse,
May bounteous heaven the feeble effort bless,
And give my simple poem wish'd success;
May beauteous nymphs, whose fascinating charm
Enchant the yielding youth with love's alarms,
Be permanent, yet let the amorous swain,
(Though she prove false,) still merciful remain.

MORNING WINTER PIECE.

Written one Morning in a Cart-shed, on the Author finding his Limbs covered with Snow, blown through the Crevices.

 What a striking scene's displayed,
  Winter with his freezing train,
 Verd'rous fields in white arrayed,
  Snow-drop whiteness decks the plain.

 See the wond'rous pow'r of heav'n,
  Operating here below,
 While, by boist'rous winds are driv'n,
  Tow'ring piles of glist'ning snow.

Peasants by the rich employed,
    Cut out paths for public good,
Lest man's precious life's destroyed,
    Lost 'midst snow or spreading flood.

' Poor men view rich friends auspicious
    Who, their drooping hearts to cheer,
Spread the board with food delicious,
    And with choice domestic beer. '

May kind gentry, bliss enjoying,
    Blest with virtues dwell secure,
Free from direful foes annoying,
    Free from hardships I endure.

Sure thought I, when wak'd this morning,
    I'm with trials quite replete,
Ere Aurora's light is dawning,
    Snow-hills rising chill my feet.

Snow-flakes round my eyes are flying,
  Sprinkling o'er my rural bed ·
Soon I'll rise—'tis dang'rous lying—
  No close curtains screen my head.

Straw's my couch, no sheets nor bedding,
  Pond'rous snow dissolving lies,
When I wake no carpet treading,
  Fleecy snow its place supplies.

No grand tap'stry decorating
  These drear walls now moist with snow,
Nought my spirits exhilarating,
  Doom'd alas to pungent woe.

In aerial regions hovering,
  Keenly chill'd in exigence,
Plumed tribes retire for cov'ring,
  No shrill matins here commence.

I forsake my snow-deck'd pillow,
  Traverse snow-enamel'd vales,
Zephyrs whisp'ring o'er the willows,
  Soon advance to flatuous gales.

Limpid dews, with gelid feature,
  Silver o'er the glist'ning scene,
'Tis not tinsell'd art,—but nature
  Speaks heaven's power in climes terrene.

Pierc'd by hunger's dart I wander,
  Trackless knee-deep snow pervade,
Cheer'd not by the rill's meander,
  View no florid sylvan shade.

Snow which Boreal blasts are whirling
  Rapid through the ambient air,
'Gainst my sordid vestment hurling,
  Dim my eyes and chill my hair.

This vile raiment hangs in tatters—
   No warm garment to defend,
O'er my flesh the chill snow scatters—
   No snug hut, nor social friend.

Though by cold severe I perish,
   No warm viands friends impart,
No rich cordial wine to cherish,
   Or revive my languid heart.

Here in vernal hours I strayed,
   Fields and limpid torrents view'd,
Splendid prospects here surveyed,
   Cheering solace then insur'd.

Plumed choirs were sweetly singing
   Anthems of celestial praise,
Soaring larks their flight were winging,
   Pleas'd melodious notes to raise.

Fulgent lustre Sol displaying,
    Brighten'd all the azure sky,
With his glorious light conveying
    Glowing lustre from on high.

Cheering all this gay creation,
    Fields and fertile vales below,
Fertilizing vegetation,
    Which does pleasing presence show.

Fain I'd gain a situation
    Quite retire, near rural shades,
There imbibe, for recreation,
    Vernal air, 'mid op'ning glades,

Florets pluck, or crop rich foliage,
    Some for drink and some to smoke,
There, when tir'd by arduous toilage,
    I'd the sylvan muse invoke.

There, assisted by Urania,
   Friends t'oblige, I'd verse compose,
Verse that might be priz'd by many
   Who adopt the theme I chose.

Heaven's rich bounty celebrating,
   I'd extol our Highest Friend,
Lenient cordials animating,
   Who t'impart does condescend.

Power supreme was erst exerted,
   Flaming bolts in Ether roll'd,
Minds terrene with fear then started—
   Now recoil at winter's cold.

Bursts terrific, vivid flashes,
   At heaven's fiat sound or shine,
Ice-like morsels, rime like ashes,
   Scatter'd forth by power divine.

Flakes of snow like wool descending
    From dense clouds yon lawn o'erspread,
With nocturnal hoar-frost blending,
    Grain's preserv'd, well covered.

Friends who wish in peaceful station
    Herbs t'amass, much good to do,
Patient wait for vegetation,
    While conceal'd beneath the snow.

Soon yon luminary shining
    Snow will melt on orient hills,
To its radiant warmth resigning,
    Praise resounds from tuneful rills.

Soon yon landscapes, groves, and bowers,
    Will a brighter verdure wear,
Rich parterres, expanding flowers,
    All in lovely hue appear.

Drinks salubrious then preparing,
   Seek a neighbour's joy and health,
Kind supernal favors sharing,
   Far transcending India's wealth.

Let's attend to truth and reason,
   While we snow-form'd mounds pervade,
Our Great Donor, in their season,
   All things beautiful has made.

Winter, Summer, still returning,
   Order'd are by sov'reign power,
Grief's sad sighs, and tears of mourning,
   Cease, and bring the joyful hour.

There serenely acquiescing,
   On rich Providence depend,
May our hearts, true grace possessing,
   With most grateful praise ascend.

Rest in solid peace and pleasure,
 Aided by celestial love,
Still aspire when brighter treasure
 Shines in blissful courts above.

There no gelid thrillings enter;
 There's a rich exhaustless store;
There, aspiring to their centre,
 Saints the great Supreme adore.

Light supernal all pervading,
 They to bright perfection come,
Vital coronets unfading
 Flourish in eternal bloom.

EVENING WINTER PIECE.

FIRST PART.

One evening walking in winter time,
The fields were overspread with hoary rime,
The snow did with inclemency descend,
While I seem'd quite forlorn, without a friend;
Some serious thoughts at length came in my mind,
Reflecting on the frailty of mankind:
Thought I, I'm but a reptile on this earth,
A scene of sorrow from my very birth,
Like other mortals I must soon decay,
And subject am to death—that dreary way;

Yet boasting man in splendour would appear,
But death a period puts to his career:
That ghastly king his harbinger doth send,
To warn vain man of his approaching end!
Then happy those, who when they hence remove
Have an eternal mansion fix'd above:
But leaving things divine above the skies,
On the chilling fleece do turn my eyes,
And meditate while in the fields I range,
How winter does the vegetables change.
Methought I walk'd last summer in this place,
Bright Phœbus had begun his morning race,
The tow'ring trees were dress'd in lovely green,
With leafy ornaments to grace the scene,
The winged tribe their cheerful notes did raise
In cheerful accents sound celestial praise,
The lark arose, and with his mounted wings
To the expansive sky ascending sings,

The fields were cover'd with the well-topp'd corn,

Rich verdure did the smiling meads adorn,

The air perfumed was with fragrancy

From the expanding flowers growing by,

Which sweetly blooming in a pleasant vale,

The languid spirits often might regale;

Bright Sol seem'd loath to leave the splendid sight,

And when he did 'twas always late at night,

But frequently rose early in the morn,

To spread his lustre o'er the verdant lawn,

The fields were glittering with the limpid dew,

While Zephyrs fann'd ambrosial spices through,

This pleasing scene delightful was to view;

The industrious bees improv'd the morning hours,

Extracting honey from the springing flowers,

And sip mellifluous dews from tender plants,

To be reserv'd in store for future wants;

The emmets toiling with incessant care,

For this cold season viands did prepare:

This is a lesson meet for us to learn,

That we through grace true wisdom may discern,

May I their school frequent, their pupil be,

Be wise in time, and for eternity.

The summer did the peaceful mind delight,

But now alas the scene is alter'd quite,

The trees disrob'd of all their rich attire,

Which in that season many did admire,

Their naked limbs to winter's rage expos'd,

While springs and rivulets by the frost are clos'd;

All nature now a dreary aspect wears,

Bright Sol's withdrawn and Cynthia disappears,

The plumed throng, which with melodious notes,

In Summer warbled in their pleasant throats,

Sit now in silence on the chilling spray,

And seem for the returning spring to pray;

The fields and meadows in the lovely spring
Seem'd with their copious crops to smile and sing,
Enamell'd with rich fragant flowers gay,
In the invigorating month of May,
Which then appear'd in all their blooming hue,
While Sol's meridian beams were darting through;
'Twas pleasant walking in the sylvan shade,
But soon these variegated flowers must fade;
The scorching sun and boist'rous wind came o'er,
The place its real owner knows no more;
O'er fields and plains an icy dew appears,
And for their loss they seem in floods of tears.
A monitor is here for giddy youth,
Who scorn the paths of piety and truth;
How many though most fair and comely made,
Yet soon their bloom decline, their beauty fade,
An icy damp those tender limbs may seize,
And soon divest them of their health and ease.

Ah! how absurd the way of death to chose,
And things divine in sad oblivion lose!
Death, like the inclement frost, may come in haste,
And cut them off as with a sudden blast,
The soul must then as sure as now they breathe,
Mount up to Heaven, or sink to Hell beneath!
Shall with the ransom'd saint in glory sit,
Or be consign'd to the infernal pit.
May I in time repent, converted be,
That all my sins I blotted out may see,
For nought but sin and sorrow here I find,
No solid joy to ease my tortur'd mind;
Where are the lenient cordials, to impart
Their healing virtues to a wounded heart?
There is a Saviour who does heal each wound
In humble souls, where'er true faith is found,
Disarms the grisly tyrant of his sting,
  And tunes the voice the Conqueror's song to sing.

Death where's thy sting? and where's thy victory grave?

I'll triumph in my Jesu's power to save!

Death's sting is sin, he drew it out alone,

When he for contrite sinners did atone.

They who through grace in virtue persevere,

Whene'er the summons come they need not fear;

Death's a kind messenger, safe to convey

Their souls to realms of never-ending day!

But some may seem the gospel to receive,

Yet ne'er repent, nor in the word believe:

If they too late for pard'ning mercy crave,

He who has form'd them will no mercy have;

Then let us humbly supplicate for faith,

To make us happy both in life and death.

EVENING WINTER PIECE.

SECOND PART.

But now another thought does strike my mind,
An emblem of the Christian here I find,
He's oft in Scripture call'd a fruitful tree,
But yet how little fruit we sometimes see;
He many trying seasons here does know,
While passing through this wilderness below,
And many sore temptations must withstand,
Ere his arrival at the promis'd land;
When Spring appears; the Sun of Righteousness
Arises and does all his wants redress

On those who fear his name Christ will arise

And give a foretaste of enduring joys,

To dissipate their fears, their doubts dispel,

And make them hate the sins that in them dwell;

And now by each discerning eye are seen

The leaves of his profession fresh and green,

Not all the measures envious foes can take,

Tho' much they strive, one leaf can ever shake;

He like the birds in Summer now can sing,

In strains sublime, the praises of his king,

Extatic pleasure elevates his mind,

Which to impart to others he's inclin'd,

To each repentant sinner he makes known

What for his precious soul kind heaven has done,

And those around him strives to edify,

By warning them they all must shortly die,

Intreats them, while their time and health endure,

To make their calling and election sure;

He daily now frequents the Throne of Grace,

And follows holiness and solid peace,

The Bible now becomes his chief delight,

In it he studies both by day and night,

From every page he does true comfort find,

'Tis sweeter than the honey to his mind,

Not all the richest treasures of Peru

Can to his soul such consolation shew;

When he receives his mean but wholesome food

He blesses him who fills his soul with good;

If with delicious cates his table's spread

He prizes them, but more the living bread,

He views the hand that all rich blessings gave,

And lives to him who died his soul to save;

His willing mind in this glad frame would stay,

And sit and sing, and wish for endless day.

Ah! blissful state, but soon this season's gone,

With northern blasts a wint'ry storm comes on,

Perhaps his faith and patience now to try,

And teach experience which may yield him joy,

Or to chastise some lust or self-applause,

Jesus, the Sun of Righteousness withdraws,

His secret sins do now appear in view,

And frowning Justice ready to pursue,

Dense clouds and freezing storms impending seem,

His joys are vanish'd like a pleasing dream,

The Scriptures, which glad tidings had reveal'd

And glorious truths to him, are almost seal'd,

The word's insipid now,—nor can he see

Milk or strong meat his nutriment to be,

" Alas!' he cries " where's my beloved gone,

" O whither is my dearest friend withdrawn?

" Where he is now retir'd did I but know,

" To seek him whom my soul admires I'd go,

" Knew I but where his flock at noon takes rest,

" Those fears would cease which rankle in my breast;"

Thus he his well-beloved's absence mourns,
Till he with gladd'ning smiles to him returns.
The trees which shake with boist'rous blasts of wind,
Do me of this sad winter's-state remind,
But tho' the raging storms o'er them presides.
They are not dead, their roots do still abide,
And tho' the Christian meets with many a shock,
He still abides, built firm upon a rock!
Now you my friends who've had experience great,
And felt the sharpness of a winter's state,
Yet once more feel the Sun's reviving rays,
Have reason to return most grateful praise,
And tho' the winter's past, the storms are fled,
Prepare for those which may hang o'er your head;
Of all events which hasten them beware,
And of your future conduct take more care;
If ye are Christ's your storms will soon be o'er,
He'll you receive where winter is no more..

Where faithful saints, exempt from sin and pain,

Like ever blooming vital trees remain,

Where Spring endures, no foes their peace destroy,

Or heaven's supreme celestial smiles alloy,

In dulcet murmurs there while tears subside,

Pure streams of bliss extatic ceaseless glide.

THE

Wounded Soldier's Return.

The sun was just retir'd, the dews of Eve
    Their glow-worm lustre scatter'd o'er the vale,
The lonely nightingale began to grieve,
    Telling, with many a pause, his tender tale.

No clamours rude disturb'd the peaceful hour,
  And the young moon, yet fearful of the night,
Rear'd her pale crescent o'er the burnish'd tow'r,
  Which caught the parting orb's still ling'ring light.

'Twas then, where peasant footsteps mark'd the way,
  A wounded soldier feebly mov'd along,
Nor aught regarded he the soft'ning ray,
  Nor the expressive bird's melodious song

On crutches borne his mangled limbs he drew,
  Unsightly remnants of the battle's rage,
While pity in his pallid looks might view
  A helpless prematurity of age.

Then, as by sad contortions, laboring slow,
  He gain'd the summit of his native hill,
And saw the well-known prospect spread below,
  The farm, the cot, the hamlet, and the mill.

In spite of fortitude, one struggling sigh

    Shook the firm texture of his throbbing heart,

And from his hollow and dejected eye

    One trembling tear hung ready to depart.

" How chang'd" he cried, " is this fair scene to me !

    " Since last across this narrow path I went,

" The soaring lark felt not superior glee,

    " Nor any human breast more true content.

" When the fresh hay was o'er the meadow thrown,

    " Amongst the busy throng I still appear'd,

" My prowess too at harvest-time was shown,

    " When Lucy's carol ev'ry labor cheer'd.

" The scorching sun I scarcely seem'd to feel;

    " If the dear maiden near me chanc'd to rove,

" And if she deign'd to share my frugal meal,

    " It was a rich repast—a feast of love.

" 'And when at ev'ning, with the rustic's pride,

" I dar'd the sturdiest wrestlers on the green,

" What joy was mine, to hear her by my side

" Extol my vigor and my manly mien?

" Alas! no more the sprightly maid shall run

" To bid me welcome from the sultry plain,

" But her averted eye my sight shall shun,

" And all my fondest cherish'd hopes be vain.

" And you, my parents, must ye too endure

" That I should ever damp your homely mirth,

" Exist upon the pittance ye procure,

" And make you curse the hour that gave me birth?

" 'Ah! hapless hour, when at a neighbouring wake,

" The gaudy serjeant caught my wond'ring eye,

" And as his tongue of war and honor spake,

" I felt a wish to conquer or to die.

" Then while he bound the ribbands on my brow,
" He talk'd of Captains kind, and Generals good
" Said a whole nation would my fame avow,
" And bounty call'd the purchase of my blood.

" But I refus'd that bounty, I disdain'd
" To sell my service in a righteous cause,
" For to my dull sense it was explain'd,
" The cause of honor, justice, and the laws.

" The rattling drums beat loud, the fifes began,
" My King and Country seem'd to ask my aid,
" Through ev'ry vein the thrilling ardor ran,
" I left my homely cot, my village maid.

" In loathsome vessels now like slaves confin'd,
" Now call'd to slaughter in the open field,
" Now backward driv'n, like chaff before the wind
" Too weak to stand, and yet asham'd to yield

" 'Till oft repeated victories inspir'd
" With tenfold fury the indignant foe,
" Who closer still advanc'd as we retir'd,
" And laid our proudest boasted honors low.

" Through burning deserts now compell'd to fly,
" Our bravest legions moulder fast away,
" Thousands, of wounds and sickness left to die,
" While hovering ravens mark'd them for their prey.

" Ah! sure remorse their savage hearts must rend
" Whose selfish desperate phrenzy could decree,
" That in one mass of murder man should blend,
" Who sent the slave to fight against the free.

" Unequal contest! at fair Freedom's call
" The lowliest hind glows with celestial fire,
" She rules, directs, pervades, and orders all,
" And armies at her sacred glance expire.

While some supinely dose on downy beds,
It folds the copper, melts the yielding lead,
Eradicates tall trees, or strikes them down,
Shatters the coach ere it arrives at town.
How dare we slumber when supernal power
Is going forth in that tremendous hour?
At the Metropolis, my courteous friend,
Much damage did this dismal storm attend,
Grand houses, walls, and chimnies were thrown down
And many precious lives were lost in town,
A painful task 'twould be, could I relate
These horrors, or the sufferers numerate,
I trust my friends, you'll not my verses scorn,
While thus I treat on that tremendous morn:
Some in the country did much loss sustain,
So dreadful was the thunder, hail, and rain,
Thousands of Pounds were lost by sea and land,
Yet 'twas the work of an Almighty hand;

The eve preceding, in my devious way,
I spied a lonely farm called Horksley-hey;
The gentry with benevolence possest,
Gave me permission there awhile to rest,
But growing late ere Cynthia gave her light,
They me permitted there to sleep that night,
Each menial servant kindly to me spake,
One shew'd me where I quiet rest might take,
But while I slumber'd in my rural bed
A sable cloud the spangled sky o'erspread,
And thus presag'd a dire impending storm;
While I seem'd shelter'd there, secure from harm,
The livid lightning blaz'd from yonder sky,
Loud thunder's voice resounded from on high,
A clap of thunder woke me with surprise,
While vivid flashes darted to my eyes,
A sudden tremor seiz'd my throbbing breast,
Sleep left my eyes, fear chas'd away my rest;

For mercy I began to supplicate,
And on the last Great Day to meditate,
But in my study could small solace find,
Such dread ideas vex'd my thinking mind;
Thought I if seated in this lone recess,
Nocturnal scenes my spirits thus depress,
If in the silent shades of gloomy night
A sudden lucid flash does thus affright,
More frightful far when sulph'rous flames descend,
And put to sublunary things an end;
If sounds of thunder so distress my ears,
And fill my mind with such foreboding fears,
How awful when the Archangel's trump shall sound,
And mould'ring corses rise from teeming ground;
The dreary scene gives no supreme delight,
Yet soar my muse, portray the amazing sight!
What horrors seize poor guilty trembling souls
When sounds terrific shake the adverse poles!

In vain to rocks or hills for aid they flee,

Bright heavens recede, this earth dissolv'd must be:

Thus when I see the lightnings blaze around,

And hear the alarming thunder's awful sound,

When hail or rain like bursting cataracts pour,

I fear 'twill strike me dead to be no more;

But flashes cease, to sooth my panic fear,

The distant sound salutes my list'ning ear.

Thus I'm permitted longer to remain

In this vain world of sorrow, sin, and pain,

This storm's a warning from the great Supreme,

That man the fleeting moments may redeem,

To one it speaks to rise and leave the dust,

Dismiss my fears, and in the Saviour trust,

Calls us to hear the bless'd inviting sound,

While free rich grace and mercy may be found.

May we through faith attend the call divine,

The joys and cares of flesh and sense resign,

Renounce our sins, or fancied righteousness,
To be invested with a glorious dress;
There, should loud thunders roll, or tempests roar,
They'll waft us nearer to the peaceful shore,
Where death and sin and sorrow are no more,
Where bright celestial day shall banish fears,
Extatic bliss succeed to flowing tears.
May this, my friends, our happy portion be,
May we be taught from wrath divine to flee,
Taught to surmount by faith all things terrene,
T'aspire to bright realities unseen,
While in the atmosphere dread thunders roar,
Revere th' Eternal, wonder, and adore.

ON THE

Death of Lord Nelson.

See in sable robes arrrayed,
    Mourners drear the streets parade;
Beaux who life's gay scenes displayed,
    Seek retir'd the sylvan shade.

Belles for dress superb admired,
    Rob'd in silks of Persian dye,
Sable vestment has attired,
    Cries excite the rising sigh.

Mourning dress succeeds to fashion,

    Sadness reigns from shore to shore,

Sorrow glooms the illumin'd nation,

    Brave Lord Nelson is no more.

Tars by storms or foes surrounded,

    His grand fiat erst obey'd,

Sympathiz'd with him when wounded,

    But his exit more dismay'd.

Many victories fam'd in story

    Gallant Nelson did acquire,

But the last with zeal for glory,

    Did each loyal mind inspire.

Britons, mourn the destin'd hour,

    When the grisly tyrant's dart

Came, and with resistless power

    Pierc'd great Nelson's thrilling heart.

From the summit or the centre
    Of a ship, the Gallic foe
Fir'd a musket at a venture,
    Gave the dread—the murd'rous blow.

Though a baleful scene appeared,
    He declar'd while life remain'd,
All his languid pow'rs were cheered,
    By the wond'rous conquest gain'd.

See kind friends in state preparing
    To inter the breathless form,
With fraternal heroes sharing
    Mansions free from boist'rous storm.

Pomp terrene behold displaying,
    See reclines the slumb'ring clay,
Till heaven's voice supreme obeying
    It revive in brilliant day.

For their loss though Britons languish,
  Limpid tears those cheeks bedew,
Let these thoughts elude dire anguish,
  His enobled mind was true.

Yet the pearly drops still flowing,
  Sprinkle o'er the hero's urn,
Loyal breasts still ardent glowing,
  Love's pure flame will fervid burn.

Albion's Sons who thus deploring,
  Bathe in tears the languid eye,
Still the blest supreme adoring,
  Hope aspires beyond the sky.

There no fluctuating surges
  With velocious fury roll,
Sanguine raiment, doleful dirges,
  Wound not the heroic soul.

There no direful arm awaits him,
   Still exists the vital flame,
In bright realms friends hope to meet him,
   Britons sound his lasting fame.

LINES ON A

Little Black Dog

STEALING THE AUTHOR'S MEAT.

In the spring of the year eighteen hundred and one,
These thoughts struck my mind while musing alone,
How bright and serene is the sunshiny day,
The birds sweetly whistle, the lambs sport and play,
The nightingale's accents resound through the grove,
All seem to aspire to bright regions above,

The whole gay creation most beauteous appears,

And each vernal scene a bright aspect wears,

All nature declares the Creator is good,

Yet I pine with distress, and languish for food;

My thoughts could I muster, and form them in rhymes,

Of half my sharp sufferings in these trying times,

The rich who regale in their luxury and pride,

Would exert ev'ry nerve that my wants might subside,

Yet if no sympathetic compassion they shew,

I have still some kind friends that will pity my woe,

I'll to Providence trust, though I've nothing to eat,

Then a kind lady gave me a piece of good meat,

And seeing me languid, my spirits to cheer,

She drew me a mug of her good home-brew'd beer;

Being bravely refresh'd, and 'twas late in the day,

I put up my meat, and I hasten'd away;

How bright was the prospect, the trees in full bloom,

The cowslips and violets sent forth their perfume,

I gather'd them into my bag so complete,

Thought I, now I'm furnish'd with med'cine and meat,

I'll purchase three pennyworth of 'tatoes to night,

To eat with my meat, it will give me delight.

How vain are our sanguinest projects below,

What losses await us, no mortal does know;

A tradesman I met coming out of an Inn,

A short friendly intercourse soon did begin,

In this social converse I told him some rhymes,

He said he'd some hopes we should have better times;

Says he you must suffer, provision's so dear,

Will you stop and take share of a mug of good beer?

I set myself down on the stepping-block stairs,

Of the robber's approach I'd no foreboding fears,

With a morsel of bread and a draught of fine ale

Before my fresh journey myself to regale;

I took from my bag an ancient good book,

And shew'd to the tradesman, he in it did look,

The book was concerning the door of salvation,

Unlock'd by the key of regeneration;

While we with attention fresh objects pursue,

A little black dog just appeared in view,

Snatch'd the pork from my bag and soon slipt away,

Crept in a sly corner to feast on its prey;

The dog being hungry, in that starving time

To search for another piece thought it no crime,

But quickly return'd, and carried away

Four ounces of suet I bought yesterday:

The maid cried out, JIMMY, you'll have nothing to eat

A little black dog has ran away with your meat;

Said I, the dire cur seeing me off my guard,

My pork has devour'd, and stole my hog's-lard;

The dog when pursu'd did the suet resign,

And now for the future it is my design

To be more circumspect wherever I go,

Or my friends will compare me to poor patient Joe

'Tis a similar case, and we sure must grow thinner,
I'm depriv'd of my supper, and he of his dinner;
My pig's suet is safe, yet one loss I've sustain'd,
My pork is quite lost, and can ne'er be regain'd,
Yet no more I'll repine, or grieve at my cross,
Some kind recent friend will compensate my loss.

ON A

Brinded Greyhound

Carrying a Piece of Meat to the Author.

In the Summer one thousand eight hundred and eight,
I travers'd gay fields, but had no food to eat,
And having no cash, no provision could buy,
Sure ne'er was poor bard so distressed as I ;

Once near the Buck's Horns I was robb'd of my meat,
Depriv'd of my supper, severe was my fate,
'Twas in the Spring time, eighteen hundred and one,
Seven years are expir'd, yet I eat bread alone,
On hard mouldy crusts and cold water I live,
Yet hope I these mercies shall grateful receive;
An excellent Prophet had nothing to eat,
Till ravens supplied him with bread and with meat,
I've heard of a good man, 'twas poor master DODD,
Had nothing for dinner, but trusted in GOD!
Rich gentry choice viands prepar'd for grand guest,
A nice joint of mutton for dinner was drest,
A vigilant dog with rapidity enter'd,
To steal the choice meat he most daringly ventur'd,
He quickly convey'd it to poor master DODD,
Domestics all feasted, and blessed their GOD!
Kind mercy supernal my wants will supply,
Inspire me with gratitude, solace, and joy,

I'll suffer with patience, and cease to complain,
In exigence I but short time may remain,
Rising sighs I'll suppress, and bid fears subside,
Sustain'd by this motto, " kind heaven will provide:"
I enter'd a farm-house, told gentry some rhymes,
They sympathiz'd with me in these trying times,
With good bread and meat I my vitals did cheer,
Refresh'd languid spirits with good home-brew'd beer;
But though for the present well sated with meat,
That I the next evening might have more to eat,
Kind Providence order'd a brinded greyhound
To filch me a piece, then recline on the ground,
The young cur most tacit resign'd it to me;
Soon ev'ry domestic did kindly agree
That I should reserve it to eat the next day.
Thus Providence surely will fodder our way;
We should not trust in man, but in aid most divine.
'Tis best in all seasons our wills to resign.

H. 5.

For though by one dog I sustained a cross,

Another relieves and compenses my loss:

If ever poor FLY should be drove to distress,

If 'tis in my power, his wants I'll redress,

If he should be hungry and have nothing to eat,

I'll give him a bone when I've stript off the meat.

ON

MAID-SERVANT KILLING TWO CATS

Attend, while I my tale begin,

A comely maid lives at an Inn,

Her mind for cruelty so bent,

Her heart obdurate wont relent;

Her worthy master, as I hear,

Did retail brandy, rum, and beer,

And kept two lovely favorite cats,

Which oft destroy'd the mice and rats;

One disoblig'd the maid one day,

At which she hung it up straitway,

She beat it with such dauntless spite,

Poor Puss was shortly slain outright;

The other soon did her displease,

She strangled that betwixt her knees;

One cries, assuage your passion pray,

The poor dumb animal dont slay,

But soon to their extreme surprise,

Poor Puss expir'd with dismal cries,

The tim'rous maid was in a fright,

Cries she, I've slain a cat this night,

The hostler runs without his hat,

The maid, says he, has kill'd the cat;

The mistress with resentment fill'd,

Cries cruel girl, poor Puss you've kill'd,

O how could you so cruel be?

Sure such a maid I ne'er did see;

Said she ma'am be not angry pray,

'Twas just, the thieves their lives should pay,

They really did my mind displease,

By stealing butter, meat, and cheese.

ANECDOTE ON

SIR PHILIP AND HIS HE-GOAT,

OR A

Caution against Ebriety.

Ye sprightly youths who in gay splendour live,

May you instruction from these lines receive,

My simple Poem with attention read,

No longer in ebriety proceed·

The secret fact which I shall now declare,

Was at a village done in Monmouthshire;

A Curate there, it seems of birth and fame,

Did long reside, Sir Philip call'd by name,

He liv'd a calm though solitary life,
Because prohibited to take a wife,
But yet he was not then abandon'd quite
From courteous females, whom our sex delight,
A woman did her kindness thus express,
She daily came delicious food to dress,
And do those things necessity requir'd,
Yet more society he still desir'd;
And though from the fair sex he must refrain,
Because the Popish tenets him restrain,
Yet he'd not long in solitude remain,
But took a' kid, and rear'd up to a goat;
Sir Philip on this animal did doat,
The goat was loving, tractable, and kind,
Which often pleas'd his master's curious mind,
He him pursu'd, and kept him in his eye,
And in his stately room did nightly lie;

Whene'er he to his sacred duty went,

The goat accompanied with full consent,

It ran before, and leap'd o'er every stile,

Which pleasing sight oft made the Curate smile;

Ent'ring the church, the service did commence,

In which the vulgar could perceive no sense,

For 'twas perform'd in the old Latin tongue,

Which could not edify an English throng,

Meanwhile the goat in th' porch could hear and see,

Though he within must not admitted be,

By near access he heard his master's voice,

Whose pleasing accents did his heart rejoice,

While he with warmth his audience did address,

And rev'rence deep did ev'ry breast possess,

The goat contented near the steeple lay,

And knew the language too as well as they:

The service o'er, they to an Inn repair'd,

To drink and spend what cash they'd lately spar'd;

When enter'd, each one took his proper place,
Sir Philip's presence did their converse grace;
While they regal'd themselves with wine or beer,
To dissipate their fears, their spirits cheer,
The goat without, a safe asylum found,
Could sleep in peace no troubles him surround;
Sometimes they'd him invite into the room,
Nor did the yielding goat refuse to come,
His coming did exhilarate the mind
Of gentlemen to mirth jocose inclin'd,
But soon his master from the Inn retir'd,
His he-goat's company he then desir'd,
They to their neat apartment took their way,
And slept secure till the return of day:
This was continu'd for a little space
Till some vile rustics, destitute of grace,
While drinking and carousing at the Inn,
Compell'd the goat to drink, which was a sin,

The ale he drank did him intoxicate,

And as it might be in the evening late,

Passing a bridge he in the river fell;

His strange surprise no human tongue can tell,

Shiv'ring he stood awhile, his fears increas'd,

But soon reviv'd, his master's footsteps trac'd,

But form'd this resolution in his breast,

He'd for the future at a distance rest,

Until his much-lov'd master home did venture,

But never more would in the ale-house enter;

And thus you see, my friends, the brute creation,

Choice lessons give to this our sinful nation,

Lessons which may of greatest moment be,

If like the goat we can our folly see;

The goat was careful never to repeat

A crime which threaten'd him with peril great,

But man, who boasts of wisdom, skill, and art,

Repeats the crimes which often cause him smart,

Visits the place were he with much expence
Has often drown'd his reason and his sense,
Revisits daily that pernicious place,
Where liquor renders him, who's void of grace,
Less rational than the unthinking brute,
While he unheedful loves his rash pursuit.
Blush ye unthinking youths! who take delight
To riot in excess both day and night,
Ye sons of dissipation young and gay,
Who waste your precious hours in mirth and play!
You, who with pleasing admiration, view
The dire licentious course you still pursue,
Review the liquor sparkling in your bowls,
Yet how unmindful of your precious souls!
Rustics be warn'd, your folly leave, I pray,
You who sit boozing at the Inn all day,
While your poor offspring's feast is scarce a crust,
And at the limpid brook they slake their thirst;

Your frugal partner, tho' depress'd by care,

For your refreshment viands does prepare,

She waits for your return, but waits in vain,

Her husband's absence does her bosom pain,

At length you stagger home, do her deride,

Ah! miscreant vile, t'abuse a loving bride;

One species of this vice does yet remain,

Which strikes the pious mind with pungent pain,

'Tis drunkenness in one advanc'd in years,

This sin almost unparallell'd appears;

Tho' the voluptuary aged grows,

Believes the scene of death must shortly close,

And knows he cannot long continue here,

Yet in wine-bibbing still will persevere:

The unerring word declares that liars all,

That murd'rers, swearers, yea, and drunkards shall

Have no inheritance among the blest,

Where saints in never-ending glory rest.

Blush then ye drunkards, and your folly mourn,

Now to the Lord with contrite hearts return,

Mercy implore from him who reigns on high,

That he with saving grace may you supply.

May you be turn'd from all your vicious ways,

And taught to give the great Supreme the praise,

Taught to renounce your sinful course of life,

All dissipation, revelling, and strife,

Nor let it e'er be said below the sky,

A goat in prudence does vain man outvie.

THE PIG-HUNT.

Attend my kind friends to my new hunting tale,

I hope no offence if the truth I reveal,

'Tis of some brave yeomen, of honor and fame,

'Twas told me in secret, (I mention no name,)

'Tis like they regal'd with hearty good cheer,

Then set out for hunting, with hounds in career;

A Pig that pertain'd to a farmer of late,

Had stray'd in the woodlands in search of its mate,

They rode on courageous, the hounds in full cry,

Then fancied, it seems, they the hare could espy,

By shouting and echo they quick'ned their pace,

The pig then pursuing they gave it a chace,

The hounds seiz'd their victim, and doom'd it to death,

It squeak'd, kick'd, and grunted, while yielding its breath;

The huntsman cries kill him, and eat him in haste,
The hounds quite obedient soon made it their feast,
Devouring the carcase, left only the feet,
'Twas young and delicious, 'twas pleasant to eat;
But ere they had finish'd their favorite prey
The huntsmen drew nearer, and one seems to say
I think 'tis a hare, another cries tush,
'Tis a fox, I'll dismount, and take off his brush;
Convinc'd of mistakes, they soon saw and admir'd,
That the farmer's fine pig had in tortures expir'd,
Who presently being inform'd of the same,
The hounds and the hunters was ready to blame,
Excited by passion, he cries what a rig,
Instead of the hare they've kill'd my fine pig;
Is this their fine hare-hunt, a pig to be slain?
I wish they may ne'er come a hunting again:
Though gentlemen kind seem to smile at the fun,
They'll surely repay me for damage they've done,

They quickly consented the loss to repair,

The farmer contented, was eas'd of his care,

But soon some spectators the matter disclos'd,

And hearing the same I these verses compos'd,

Which plain simple lines a burlesque may appear,

But 'twas not my design these worthies to jeer,

For pigs in that season the woods much pervade,

'Tis excusable if such mistake may be made,

Yet 'twas somewhat rare, and the hounds seem'd quite
    cloy'd,

But I think 'tis a pity the pig they destroy'd,

It might have been roasted, the gentry to dine,

Their bottles and glasses o'erflowing with wine,

While they drink to brave sportsmen, and each social
    friend,

And thus, Sirs, my Pig-hunting story shall end.

LINES ON A

Gift of Coals to the Poor

BY LADY ROWLEY,

AT STOKE BY NAYLAND.

One night my mind to Colchester was bent,

And towards it to walk was my intent,

But felt a small degree of anxious pain,

Lest cold I should receive by falling rain,

Besides thought I, 'twill give me no delight,

To travel in the darksome dreary night,

Here to remain till morning will be best,

At Stoke this night I'll therefore take my rest:

I on a chamber slept at th' Angel-gate,

And as it rain'd next morn, I studied late,

Upon these trying times, did much reflect,

Thought I, tis pity some dont show respect

On their poor neighbours, times are grown so hard:

But turning now my eyes into the yard,

A pleasing sight I see this very day,

A quantity of coals to give away;

The poor who erst with penury did grieve,

Are waiting now this present to receive,

Some gentlemen appear among them too,

To see that each one has his proper due,

One of these worthies on the waggon stands,

Pen, ink, and paper seem to adorn his hands,

While I sit writing in this lone recess,

I can't attend to all they now express,

The noisy throng impedes, and stormy day;

Replete with sympathy, one seems to say

Here are poor friends whose families are large,
Which really put them to a daily charge,
Let them four bushels have, these others, two,
And these three bushels are, poor man, for you.
Methinks, these worthy gentlemen take pains
To measure out the coals while thus it rains,
Their condescension shews them void of pride,
While they the gift impartially divide,
Maids, wives, and boys, I view with bags and sacks,
Some carry home the coals upon their backs:
Females of tender frame by weight deprest,
To th' other sex, more strong, make this request,
" Convey these to my dwelling, if you please,
'Twill from my burden give me present ease;"
To carry mine, says one, I am not able,
You'll me oblige to set it in the stable,
And let it stand in safety there I pray,
Till to my cottage I the same convey;

Some jointly now agree to fill a cart,

That those who distant live may have a part,

Others to load their ponies do require,

Thus all obtain good fuel for the fire,

That those who hardly can their living earn,

Or scarce get firing for their spinning yarn,

While some small brands, a little straw, or haum,

Elude their wishes, but their limbs not warm,

May now enjoy from coals a frugal fire,

To warm their hands and feet as they desire,

To dress their wholesome food, wash, bake, and brew,

Or part reserve, lest frost should yet ensue;

Some friend beneficent, this day, 'tis said,

Supplies these neighb'ring poor with loaves of bread,

Thus they have fire to warm, and bread to eat,

The staff of life, though not o'erſed with meat;

But now another thought comes in my mind,

What bounteous hand is this that is so kind?

Though in it I've no share, yet I rejoice,

Nor listen to proud envy's scorning voice;

My mind, while unconfin'd by things of sense,

Would view the lib'ral hand of Providence!

Mysterious Providence I now recall,

Whose hand unseen does wisely order all·

That wheel of Providence, replete with eyes

Of piercing sight, each exigence espies,

Surveys the orphan's tears, the widow's grief,

Excites the wealthy to impart relief!

Kind heaven with talents does the rich intrust,

It gives delight to see them true and just,

The gifts, grand Nobles have, are only lent,

We see, sometimes, for special ends they're sent:

Thus when their hearts are taught by grace divine,

They will to hospitality incline,

Employ their precious hours in doing good,

To teach the thoughtless, give the hungry food,

To clothe the naked when in keen distress,

That their warm limbs the helping hand may bless,

Which does their grate supply with fire when old,

To warm their tender limbs now chill'd with cold.

A noble lady this donation gave,

T'assist the industrious 'poor,' who well behave;

May her successors still enjoy a fire,

And every needful blessing they desire:

May they on earth each pious wish obtain,

And then through grace in endless glory reign!

As those who o'er the poor have special care,

Susceptible of tender feelings are,

Excited by rich grace and love divine,

May ev'ry heart to gratitude incline.

ON THE OPENING OF

A NEW PEAL OF EIGHT BELLS,

THE GIFT OF

The Right Honorable the Earl of Dysart.

 One Monday, though a show'ry day,
  And in the afternoon,
 For Helmingham I urg'd my way,
  'Twas on the tenth of June:—

 Of but one halfpenny possest,
  Nor had I broke my fast,
 My spirits languid and deprest,
  I needed some repast.

A rural farm affords a friend,
    Who shelters me from rain,
And kindly does assistance lend,
    To sooth keen hunger's pain.

The verdant meadows I pervade,
    Where plumed choirs are singing,
Gay florets deck the sylvan shade,
    And op'ning bells are ringing.

The garden near yon sacred place,
    Grand gentry does contain,
Attended there by ev'ry grace,
    They're seen in sprinkling rain.

Ladies adorn the brilliant scene,
    Drest in superb attire,
With fine umbrellas, blue or green,
    While gazing groups admire!

Near the church portal I espy'd,
  A famous Flying Boat,
Brisk children lov'd aloft to ride,
  Or in mild air to float.

I traverse now amidst the throng,
  The consecrated ground,—
Some in the Park attune a song,
  While dulcet notes rebound.

In this vicinity I hear
  Some special ringers dwell,
Others from Norwich too, appear,
  'Tis thought their notes excel!

They on delicious viands dine;
  Then take their turns to ring,
They drink, in luscious punch or wine,
  "Success to Earl and King."

The Noble Earl does condescend

 With menials to converse,

And will commence the peasant's friend

 If he his bale rehearse.

Whene'er a noble Lord benign,

 Choice favours does impart,

I hope inferiors will incline

 To shew a grateful heart.

Ere animating scenes do close,

 They thus express their joys,

Round yon Parterre the sprightly beaux

 Draw him with great applause.

In a Marquee some gentry meet,

 On rich provisions dine,

While glasses, with choice wine replete,

 Do most translucent shine.

Rich cates that deck the festive board,
    The curious taste, invite,
While stalls, with various dainties stor'd,
    Give rustic minds delight.

Here, with delicious fruit I meet,
    And there, with wholesome cheer,
This cask, with spirits is replete,
    And that, with good old beer.

But soon the liquor's all drank out,
    Such numbers grace the park,
Rustics and beaux begin to doubt,
    They'll have no more till dark.

Innkeepers soon into the park
    Convey'd more beer and gin,
At ev'ry booth, before 'twas dark,
    They welcom'd Yeomen in.

Then passing by green leafy bow'rs,
    Form'd by tall spreading trees,
Where gentry spend bright vernal hours
    Of elegance and ease.

I, Yeomen brave, who form a row,
    With grand drest Ladies, view;
Those fine umbrellas splendid show,
    Ting'd with an azure hue.

Behold, on yonder eminence,
    The barrel flows with beer,
Supplies the throng, without expense,
    Their drooping hearts to cheer.

Bibacious, sordid louts draw near,
    And drink while some do spill,
Some leave the place and get no beer,
    While others drink their fill.

O'er verdant grass the sportive deer
    Each other frisk and bound,
I to the spacious Hall draw near,
    Where gliding streams surround.

I thought by leave to enter there,
    A worthy friend to find,
The bridge recedes ere I get near,
    No solace cheers my mind.

Then near the moat some beaux I meet,
    And belles array'd in white,
I speak a verse, we kindly greet,
    And each cries out "good night."

At close of day, near to the Hall,
    The Rural Sports commence,
Thought I, I'll stay to see them all,
    Ere I retire from hence.

A *Jingling Match* does now begin,

    One of the throng they blind,

And he the prize is sure to win,

    Who does the Jingler find.

Ripe Fruit and *Cash* are now brought out,

    For which young striplings strive,

Thus ev'ry beau and ev'ry lout

    Seems pleasant and alive.

A *White Chemise* appears in view,

    For which two lasses run,

Drest up with ribbands, red and blue,

    One loves the pleasing fun.

A *Pole* is fixt, all over *greas'd*,

    Rustics to *climb* begin,

And either surely would be pleas'd,

    A genteel *Hat* to win.

The Sports are o'er,—the ev'nings' dark,
  And I with speed retire,
To seek repose I leave the Park,
  Good lodging I desire.

I to the *Greyhound* make my way,
  Refuse to enter there,
Sleep in a barn till dawning day,
  Then walk for vernal air.

This "MONDAY'S WALK" now at the Hall
  Submissive I'd present,
And hope the Lords and Ladies all
  To view it will consent.

The Author's Second Day

AT

HELMINGHAM.

On Wednesday morn, I rise and dress,
    My mind seem'd more at ease,
Think I, as I'd success last night,
    I still will strive to please.

Among the booths no more I'll rove,
    But study near the Hall,
Whose inmates are replete with love,
    And I'll oblige them all.

The does are sporting full of glee,
    While bright the Sun does shine;
I write beneath the spreading tree,
    Where servants milk their kine.

And whilst I write my friends to please
    I view the lovely fair
Walk out with elegance and ease,
    To taste the vernal air.

As through the spacious park they walk,
    Or o'er the meadows rove,
Of nature's works they seem to talk,
    Or muse on virtuous love.

Some ladies fair and gentlemen
    Enter the gliding boat,
To move for pleasure all begin
    Round the capacious moat.

The gentlemen the ladies row,
  The spacious Hall around,
While limpid streamlets gently flow,
  And bells harmonious sound.

They cry'd " you view each lovely scene,
  On this you'll rhyme a verse,"
" I'll then" said I, " howe'er so mean,
  " The pleasing tale rehearse."

Beneath the spreading shady tree
  For study I recline,
View bucks and does in sportive glee,
  While solar rays do shine.

If gentry most benign permit,
  I'll hail reviving Spring,
Beneath these leafy branches sit,
  And hear the long peal ring.

The cheerful ringers still obey
    The Noble Donor's will;
In ringing changes every day,
    They shew their strength and skill.

But now! comes on the close of day,
    Bells cease awhile to ring,
In lovely strains the music play,
    Some chaunt " God save the King."

Two special ringers I espy'd,
    A farmer and his son,
Who kindly me with cash supply'd,
    The junior thus began :—

" My Sister dear, who erst was kind,
    " While verses you compos'd,
" Lately her vital breath resign'd—
    " And death her eyelids clos'd.

" I wish you, in these vernal days

" An Elegy to write;"

" I'll strive, kind Sir, your mind to please,

" And wish you both good night."

Now courteous friends, I've told the tale,

Of walking in the Spring,

To hear the cheering tuneful peal

Of bells melodious ring.

Noah's Ark.

When Noah and his family
Were warn'd the impending storm to flee,
Moved by fear, he soon did yield,
Through faith, a curious ark to build.

'Twas no vain fancy or a dream,
For God himself contriv'd the scheme,
The Lord, who form'd the wondrous plan,
To save from wrath lost guilty man.

Rain caus'd the waters to increase,
Till God commanded it to cease;
Noah, the good effects to prove,
Sent first a raven, then a dove.

The raven soon the earth possest,
The harmless dove could find no rest,
But sought the Ark with seeming pain,
Then kindly was receiv'd again.

Once more the turtle left its mate,
To see if waters did abate,
Brought back an olive branch of peace,
Which caused Noah's fears to cease.

The raven seems to earth inclin'd,
An emblem of the carnal mind,
Which grovels in the sordid dust,
And scorns in Christ alone to trust.

The dove's an emblem of the mind
That's humble, patient, and resign'd,
To dove-like minds, by fears deprest,
The world and sin can give no rest.

The seeking soul each refuge tries,
Till wing'd by faith to Christ she flies,
And finds, which makes her fears to cease,
In him a true—a solid peace.

All false foundations saints despise,
Nor trust to refuges of lies,
Christ is their Ark, he firm remains,
'Midst floods of vengeance he sustains.

Lord, teach poor sinners now to fly
To that sure refuge, ere they die,
That when their breath they shall resign,
Their souls may rise to joys divine. A.

Verses

Written in Great Bealings Churchyard,

DESCRIPTIVE OF THE

SCENERY NEAR THE CHURCH.

While I the muse invoke in smiling Spring,
   Near Bealiugs Church in solitude I stray,
   Where Christians meet, devoutly sing and pray,
Revere their God, honour our gracious King.

In the Churchyard I view each sculptur'd tomb,
   Mortals in silent graves reclining rest,
   And may their spirits shine among the blest,
Now all their generation work is done.

I view the tow'ring trees in even row ;

   Gentry behold them distant near a mile,

  A view of those may fleeting hours beguile,

While limpid streamlets murmur down below.

Here courteous Ladies walk for vernal air,

   While Phœbus sheds o'er all a lucid ray,

   The azure skies a beauteous scene display,

And meads enamell'd are with flowrets fair.

At the declivity of yonder hill,

   The chesnut trees there make a fine display,

   There sheep and bleating lambkins play,

While water glides in yon meandering rill.

The Shepherd comes, the morn's serene and fair,

   The dew-bespangled meads are spread with sheep,

   Brisk lambs are sporting on the mountain steep,

O'er whom he watches with a guardian's care.

Some turn the glebe and hail the rosy morn,
> With carrots one supplies the prancing steed,
> Or with potatoes steers and heifers feed,
Some separate the thistles from the corn.

Methinks loud female accents I discern,
> Women and maids their servile station fill,
> They sort potatoes near the rising hill,
And cut them in the new-erected barn.

If these are planted in a fertile field,
> Well cultivated, then reserv'd in store,
> And vended to accommodate the poor,
With grateful hearts they'll nutriment receive.

A florid scene attracts my curious eye,
> A spacious garden with parterres replete,
> Where sportive zephyrs fan th' ambrosial sweet
From flowers expanding in most lovely dye.

Here lilachs bloom superb in gaudy pride,
    And bright laburnums also tow'ring high,
    Which seem aspiring toward the lofty sky,
While tulips, turks, and daisies all subside.

Near to the shady bowers, or summer seat,
    See yon small flower array'd in snowy white,
    Which form'd in posies gentry's minds delight,
This lovely flower is humble, pure, and neat.

A wood the rustics range ere blushing morn,
    Crop this small herb in dreary shades of night,
    Recede when first they view the dawning light,
When fair Aurora does the hills adorn.

If to obtain a garden was my fate,
    As Earls and Squires this floweret do not scorn,
    But it the Ladies' bosoms does adorn,
This floweret my parterre should decorate.

Lilly-Convally is its proper name,
  This with some other flowers or herbs I'd take,
  Them pulverize, and sneezing powder make,
If heaven me bless with wealth and fame.

A noble lady did this plant forbid,
  Whene'er for it in sylvan shades they stray
  If they're detected in meridian day,
'Tis taken from them, and they're sharply chid.

But I, perhaps, may kind reception meet,
  To take it from me would my spirits grieve,
  So should I go I'd ask the gentry's leave,
My bags should both with lilies be replete.

But if to my request they'll not consent,
  To Lilly-wood in Essex I'll repair,
  And gather plenty of May-lilies there,
And in that neighbourhood a verse present.

A noble lord is owner of this farm,

  Might I presume, I would a favour crave,

  That I a pleasant cot built up might have,

Where I could muse and study free from harm.

LINES MADE BY THE AUTHOR

WHEN A LITTLE BOY,

On a Journey with his Father to Wicken Hall

Good Sir, I most grateful and thankful would be

For all your kind favors and presents to me,

As I'd from my infancy heard of your fame,

I anxious appear'd till to see you I came;

One evening my father unto me did say,

To-morrow at Wicken a visit we'll pay,

To a gentleman there, of benevolent mind,

With affluence bless'd, and by knowledge refin'd,

The name Jimmy Chambers he sometimes does hear,

And wishes to see you as we live so near.

To this kind proposal I soon did consent,

Next morning alert with my father I went,

But ere we got half way, I thought it so far,

That surely the end of the world must be there;

Fine prospects appear'd to our view on the right,

A neat little city our theme did invite;

The fam'd Ely minster did lofty appear,

Besides we'd a view of three mills and Soham Mere;

Your church and your steeple I did'nt much admire,

Because I was certain our own was much higher.

Your house I could view, Sir, above all the rest,

And there I was likely for to fare the best;

You receiv'd me as well as I e'er could desire,

With the Miss's company and a good fire;

You gave me plum-pudding, which pleased me well,

And other good food, that I might have my fill;

You gave me strong beer, in a fine silver cup,

I grateful receiv'd it, with joy drank it up:

I walk'd in the garden, and sweet cooling shade,

Miss Nancy and I quite alertly there play'd,

Then sat in the parlour, with hearts full of glee,

Regaling on toast, with fine coffee and tea;

You gave me a coat, Sir, which home I did take,

A coat and a waistcoat and small-clothes to make,

Which when I put on in the time of the Spring,

When the dirt is dried up, and the cuckoo does sing,

I'll take a fresh journey to shew you how fine

I shall be in this neat apparel of mine.

ON THE
BENEVOLENCE OF A FRIEND.

At eve I walk'd in keen distress,
    In yonder town, disturb'd in mind;
Kind friends, who might my grief redress,
    I at the present could not find.

Friends yield no solace—not the least,
    No gentry for my help provide,
But like the Levite and the Priest,
    They pass by on the other side.

At dusky eve, returning home,
    Directed by kind Providence,
A gentleman did near me come,—
    Is this, thinks he, a man of sense?

He walk'd and talk'd with me awhile,
>Our sentiments seem'd well to agree;
Thus we the moments did beguile,
>Then he compassion had on me.

He took me to the *Falcon* Inn,
>Where he my drooping heart did cheer,
And tho' devoid of punch or gin,
>Regal'd on biscuits and old beer.

He pitied there my case forlorn,
>How I subsisted could not see,
To purchase viands in the morn,
>An argent piece he gave to me.

Surely this worthy gentleman,
>That ev'ning, so benignly kind,
Resembles the Samaritan,
>Who erst the poor man's wound did bind.

He plac'd him on his yielding beast,
    And entertain'd him at an Inn,
Defray'd the expences of the feast—
    Beneficence he thought no sin.

Such is the neighbour, this the friend,
    The Saviour teaches us to love,
Who does such kind assistance lend—
    But there's a special friend above.

A friend, celestial and divine,
    Who lenient cordials does impart,
Consoles with oil, and cheers with wine,
    The baleful Christian's languid heart.

VERSES ON

Grundisburgh Fair.

On Whitsun-Monday was a Fair,
Gay Ladies bright assembled there,
'Twas on a pleasant rural green,
Where gentlemen to walk were seen,
While nature bloom'd in gaudy pride,
To deck the scene at Whitsuntide.

Bright Sol emits a lucid ray,
'Tis a serene and pleasant day;
Some did the verdant meads pervade,
And to their friends a visit paid,
Young females walk for vernal air,
Their sweethearts meet at Whitsun Fair.

Most courteous they young ladies treat,
And buy them luscious fruit to eat,
Then at the *Dog*, or *Half Moon* drink,
The reck'ning pay in ready chink;
The Yeoman, with his much-lov'd bride,
Walks to the Fair at Whitsuntide.

The peasant's wife her cottage leaves,
A penny for her offspring saves,
Does for each child a fairing buy,
With nuts and cakes does them supply,
While beaux for rural sports provide,
The Fair to adorn at Whitsuntide.

Rude boys, whose hands were fast'ned tight,
Strove hard some treacled rolls to bite;
A Jingling Match did then begin,
That one a genteel Hat might win,
Several to catch the Jingler try'd,
But one prevail'd at Whitsuntide.

A Donkey-race too there was seen;
Two asses ran on yonder green,
Rustics then for sweet lumps did run,
While gazing lowns laugh'd at the fun,
The winners thus were well supply'd,
With dulcet cates at Whitsuntide.

The lads who lucky were to win,
Might social meet at yonder Inn,
There, as the beverage was sweet,
All slake their thirst—in union greet,
With porter, wine, or good old beer,
At Whitsuntide, their hearts to cheer.

Methinks I hear these words resound
From pious Christians dwelling round,
I vain amusements do not love,
Of sacred writings I approve,
With choice provisions I'm supplied,
I'll feast at home at Whitsuntide.

To visit Fairs I'm not inclin'd,

The noise and bustle hurt my mind,

There fleering lowns, who without cause,

Will break the peace and wholesome laws,

While worthies grand in chariots ride,

And peace enjoy at Whitsuntide.

I feel no real pure delight,

To riot in excess all night,

It me enerves, it gives me cold,

'Tis neither good for young or old;

Should heaven a peaceful home provide,

I'd there repose at Whitsuntide.

Not long I'd tarry at a Fair,

Unless I'd special business there,

Or with a friend to stop and dine,

And cheer my languid heart with wine,

At home then supper to provide,

I'd leave gay scenes at Whitsuntide.

Some Christians shun a nightly Fair,
And say there works of darkness are,
Ebriety and fornication
Abound in this our christian nation,
Blasphemy, luxury, and pride,
Disgrace the Fairs at Whitsuntide.

I hope, my friends each vice will cease,
And Fairs and Markets not disgrace,
That virtues in their stead may reign,
And discord ne'er our bosoms pain,
With plenty may we be supplied,
And peace enjoy at Whitsuntide.

The Poor Poetaster.

I, the poor Poetaster, bewail my hard fate,
Sad losses and cares have depress'd me of late,
My cash is dispers'd, friends seem to turn foes,
I've walk'd till I'm weary, and worn out my clothes.
My stockings are torn as I walk in the dirt,
And some months I've existed without any shirt
My feet they go wet, and my neck catches much cold,
And rustics despise me because poor with and old;
As to pay for a bed I've of late not been able,
By permission I've slept on some straw in a stable;
Friends lent me a cloth to preserve me from harm,
In sharp freezing weather I sometimes lie warm;

I lodg'd in a calf's-crib by leave of a friend,
Gelid snow and short straw did promiscuously blend;
The boys did insult me, they filched my store,
They my property spoil—'tis my fate to be poor.
From place then to place I was harass'd about,
Ston'd, robb'd, and insulted by every base lout;
While I was at Church they play'd a sad joke,
They stole all my nets, and my pitcher they broke;
I mov'd to a whin-shed, 'twas worse still indeed,
They filch'd my good books, now I've not one to read;
Into a cold pig-stye I sometimes did creep,
Undress'd me, and by are on the damp floor did sleep,
Stones came in t   , and snow in the night,
Which hurt me a   kill'd me, forbidding delight,
Dire foes to insult me exerted their spite;
When under a corn-hole I often reclin'd,
There with a low ceiling was nightly confin'd,

A bed in the straw-stack I make down below,

The rain pour'd upon me—I'm sprinkled with snow:

Ye gentry, who on a soft down bed repose,

Consider poor bards who in gelid air dose;

On Sunday when I to sacred courts went,

Louts and morts, to filch from me, the precious hours spent;

Again in the hog's cote I slept among strife,

Was mobb'd out of town, and escap'd for my life;

In barns I'm surrounded too oft by the mob,

And slyly they enter, they spoil and they rob.

A farmer of late was to me very kind,

For in his new building by leave I reclin'd;

, by a dire scold, was chas'd out with all speed,

As they wanted the place the turkies to feed;

By hurry and bustle my money I lost,

'm cashless and starving—how poor bards are cross'd;

My writings I lately had dropp'd near the yard,
Of them I've not heard—sure my fate it is hard;
In a large open shed I reclin'd day and night,
The muse to invoke, to rhyme verses, and write;
In a waggon I take my nocturnal repose,
No covering alas! but my old tatter'd clothes,
No blanket nor rug, me to screen from the storm,
Keen pinching air breathes—how can one lay warm
My sufferings are grievous in these trying times,
Though noted for making and speaking of rhymes,
And tho' some friends in Suffolk still kindly behave
Yet I'm so reduc'd, I this county must leave,
Yet favours I'd prize, and most grateful would be
To gentry benign, who shew kindness to me;
If life should permit, soon to Ipswich I'll go,
In search of new friends, and to Colchester too:
Good Christians, no doubt, of compassionate heart,
Will sympathize with me—choice favours impart;

Should schemes prove abortive, to Cambridge I'll go,

Relate my sad tale of ineffable woe,

Perhaps I a weekly collection may find,

My frame to sustain, and to sooth my sad mind:

If Providence kind, recent friends does not raise,

I in a dread workhouse must finish my days,

Must cease turning verses, and noding choice twine,

While some fellow-mortals in these branches shine.

'Tis true workhouse rulers plain viands prepare,

And paupers industrious in wholesome food share,

A hot dinner three times a week they provide,

Good pudding and meat, and some butter beside,

Each one that's mature has a pint of small beer,

Of ale each a pint, three or four times a year;

Half a bed on a garret, with covering warm,

Would there be my lot, to defend me from harm,

By day I must dwell where there's many a wheel,

And a female's employ'd to sit down and reel,

A post with two ringles is fix'd in the wall,
Where orphans when lash'd, loud for mercy do call;
Depriv'd of fresh air, I must there commence spinner,
If I fail of my task, I lose a hot dinner;
Perhaps at the whipping-post then shall be flogg'd,
And lest I escape my leg must be clogg'd,
While tyrants oppress I must still be their slave,
And cruelly used, though well I behave:
'Midst swearing and brawling my days I must spend,
In sorrow and anguish my life I must end:
Of this cruelty I've had experience before,
And wish, their keen lash to come under no more;
The young, they encourag'd the old to abuse,
They both youth and age do inhumanly use,
Friendless orphans they beat, while for mercy they cry'd,
The blood it gush'd forth—they in agony dy'd,
Dropp'd down on the floor, no more did they rise,
Which struck timid minds with a sudden surprise;

I too was abus'd, 'twill again be the case,
If a great happy change has not taken place:
For numbers of years I have verses compos'd,
In hopes to find solace, ere life shall be clos'd,
A baleful requital for all labours past
Twill be, if in prison I breathe out my last;
If I must submit, then farewell blooming trees,
Farewell gliding streamlets, and zephyr's soft breeze;
now bid adieu to the cool sylvan shades,
Adieu! tuneful muses, and fine florid glades,
Farewell all connections in country and town!
Farewell worthy gentry, of fame and renown!
Kind neighbours farewell! you no more will me see,
If those direful mansions reserv'd are for me;
But sure wealthy friends, when they see I look old,
And view my bare limbs thus expos'd to the cold,
Replete with philanthropy soon will be kind,
Impart some relief to compose my sad mind,

Procure me a dwelling-place and a good fire,
With all needful blessings, this life can desire,
I then would not envy the rich nor the great,
But strive to prepare for a more blissful state.
I wish for a garden, fruit trees, and a vine,
And though on coarse viands and herbage I dine,
Secure in my dwelling none dare me molest,
A hymn I'd compose, in tranquillity rest;
The Scriptures I'd search, which are worthy esteem,
And moments most precious I'd strive to redeem;
Rich grace and free mercy should then be my theme,
In bright vernal hours—when by power divine,
Sol's clear fulgid rays most pellucid shall shine;
When gay florid scenes decorate fertile fields,
Meads beauties display—each bright scene solace yields,
When cheer'd plumed choirists their dulcet notes raise,
In accents melodious chant heaven's high praise,

I'd walk for fresh air in the fine open glades,

And crop precious herbs in the cool sylvan shades,

To plant in my garden, selecting the best

For chemists of art, to distil or digest;

Or anodynes form, which will give present ease,

I'd exert every nerve, the kind gentry to please.

Yet tho' worthy friends I've express'd my desire,

All hope still declines this my wish to acquire,

I'm incessantly troubled, while foes me oppress—

From gentry benign, I'd solicit redress;

From this wretched station, kind friends, me release,

Sarcasms and insults obtrude on my peace;

Confine me in prison, recluse from man's sight,

That I, like JOHN BUNYAN, experience may write,

Or study Acrostics, of various kinds,

Fair Ladies to please, and sooth gentlemen's minds;

Plain verses and sonnets in gaol I might rhyme,

The lone muse assisting, I'd thus spend my time,

Or like one in Newgate, replenish'd by Lore,

Who took a survey of America's shore,

Surmounted dire foes, and increased his store;

Or let me exist in a drear exile state,

I'd either prefer to my sufferings of late;

But rather than pass through more drear scenes of woe,

Or into some mansions of industry go,

'Mongst Belial's sons of contention and strife,

To breathe out the transient remains of my life;

In a neat market town I'll reside for awhile,

There friends t' oblige, fleeting moments beguile,

A chamber or garret I'll cease to refuse,

Like a mean Grub-street bard there in solitude muse.

VERSES ON A

RAT KNAWING TWINE,

And winding it many times round the Bed-post.

In Summer I travers'd the clear sylvan shade,
Bright Sol's lucid rays the tall branches pervade,
Rich herbage and verdure the meads still adorn,
And brisk feather'd songsters still hail the bright morn.

I wander'd,—then paus'd, and seem'd rather to fret,
Thought I, if I'd twine, I would work up a net,
Then vend it, and purchase some bread and some beer,
Tho' little for money, my spirits 'twould cheer.

To these adverse trials, ah! why was I born?
But I see yon bright fields standing thick with ripe corn,
With patience I'll suffer, and cease to repine,
To Providence trust, who is kindly divine.

Espying a Farm-house that stands quite alone,
'Twas in harvest, one thousand eight hundred and one,
I tarried awhile there, to work in a field,
Which does rich provision and medicine yield.

Still having occasion a trifle to earn,
I mov'd to another, and wrought in a barn;
Kind friends at both houses did courteous behave,
Good food, wholesome liquor, and money they gave.

As making of nets is sometimes my delight,
I set out for Lavenham, arriv'd there at night,
Repair'd to a shop, where I purchas'd some thread,
Then at a mean lodging house hired me a bed.

I wound in two bottoms nine penn'orth of twine,
Then up stairs retir'd, my poor head to recline,
One ball I secur'd but dropp'd one on the floor,
A rat all night long was plundering my store.

When day-light was dawning I soon found my thread
Dispers'd o'er the chamber, or drawn round the bed,
Some dragg'd in a hole, and some eaten in twain,
Then I hasten'd down stairs of my loss to complain.

" In minutes nocturnal" said I, " while in bed,
" The rat was destroying and spoiling my thread;
" Behold this new twine, once substantial and strong,
" 'Tis gnaw'd into pieces but three inches long.

" What a pity! why Sally, you need to keep cats:
" You lock up your victuals, and starve the poor rats;
" Thus, by their keen hunger, and preying on thread,
" I'm depriv'd of the means of procuring my bread."

" For your loss, replied Sally, " I'm sorry indeed,
" But I ne'er can afford those base vermin to feed;
" Provision of all sorts is dear, and I'm sure
" To exclude every thief I'll my cupboard secure."

" 'Tis true" resum'd I, " provision's quite dear,
" And we still need refreshment, our vitals to cheer;
" But some method adopt, the dire miscreants destroy,
" Or no peace in your cot can you hope to enjoy.

" But my loss I'll disclose, as a rat was the thief,
" Perhaps some rich christian will write me a brief,
" Fresh cash thus collecting, I'd buy some more thread
" And work up some nets to supply me with bread.

" But on friends to impose thus why should I desire,
" Or to living sublime and voluptuous, aspire?
" They merit my thanks, they've already been kind,
" I'll submit to my loss with composure of mind."

SERIOUS REFLECTIONS

ON A

Thunder Storm.

Near Blunts Wood as I sit writing,
   Solar rays with lustre shine,
Here I fain would be inditing,
   Waiting for a theme divine.

No vile fleering lowns surround me,
   I their converse ne'er approve,
No sarcastic speech confounds me,
   Silent vernal hours of love.

Fragrant flowers around me blooming,
   Deck the verdant meads and fields,
Odour rich the air perfuming,
   Which mellifluent sweetness yields.

Well-form'd ears of corn are shining,
   And the fertile fields adorn,
Soaring choirs their flight are winging,
   Mattins chant each vernal morn.

Sol sheds scorching rays most fulgid,
   Which illume the azure sky,
I've the sylvan muse indulged,
   Till dread prospects strike mine eye.

Dense clouds o'er yon woodlands rising,
   In most sable dress appear,
Thunders roar with voice surprising,
   Pleasing sounds no longer cheer.

Vivid flashes, lucid blazing,
>   To the eye velocious shine,
Rattling hail, of size amazing,
>   All declare a power divine.

Sounds and flashes keep their motion,
>   Float along the dreary space,
Hovering o'er the eastern ocean,
>   Fears in timid minds increase.

Syrens, with melodious voices,
>   Will perhaps their accents raise,
The good mariner rejoices,
>   'Midst alarms his God he'll praise.

When tremendous storms are ended,
>   And we breathe in air serene,
Praise the power which us defended,
>   Grateful view the brilliant scene.

Heaven our worthless lives has spared,
   And does special favors give,
Christians his rich grace have shared;
   May they to his glory live.

Strive to improve with aspect cheerful,
   Talents by our Donor given,
Lightnings flash, no more be fearful,
   Trust in Christ, and seek for heaven.

ACROSTIC.

(William Moore, Plumber, Glazier, and Painter.)

W inter is now receding, lovely Spring

I nvites the mind, while feather'd chorists sing,

L ively they matins chant, in smiling May,

L impid streams glide, enamell'd meads look gay;

I n this retreat how pleasant 'tis to rove,

A round the fertile fields, or tufted grove,

M using on Providence, and friendly love.

M ay will appear, her pleasing charms resume,

O 'er verdant fields the fragrant flowers will bloom,

O n mossy bank, or in the shady bower,

R etir'd then may you spend a leisure hour,

E xerting for the best each mental power.

P raise power supreme, my friend, which does impart,

L ife's health and strength with mental power alert,

U nite with friends who faithful are and kind,

M usic esteem, which may improve the mind,

B e virtuous while you lead a single life,

E lude all vicious ways, and baleful strife ;

R eplete with virtue, free from sorrows vie,

G lory ascribe to him who reigns on high,

L ife's joys he gives to all a rich supply ;

A lert let sacred notes towards heaven aspire,

Z ealous to join the bright celestial choir :

I n dulcet strains let friends their voices raise,

E xtol their Maker's name in grateful praise,

R emain still faithful in youth's blooming days.

A las ! frail man is but as brittle glass,

N ot long he has through this vain world to pass :

D elight rich Nobles take on downy bed,

P rinces, when life recedes, may sleep in lead ;

A nxious and baleful fears may hence subside,

I f you in youth chose out a virtuous bride:

N ew pleasures will succeed if nuptial bands

T wo hearts unite, and join your willing hands,

E xist in friendly peace, and mutual love,

R eplete with mercy seek rich joys above.

DOUBLE ACROSTIC.

(William Damant, Clarissa Gross.)

W inter recedes, inclement storms are o'er,
   C heerly and pleasant days appear once more,
I n verdant groves the birds do sweetly sing,
   L ively and brisk they hail reviving Spring;
L ovely and pleasant is the shady grove,
   A broad for pleasure now young lovers rove;
L ovely gay florets, which the meads pervade,
   R eplete with charms appear, yet soon will fade,
I f scorching rays, or boisterous blasts come o'er,
   I nviting flowerets fade, they're seen no more;
A dorn'd with beauties, and with charms most rare,
   S erene and pleasing seems the lovely fair,
M odest and gentle, affable, and kind,
   S uch are the charms which deck the virtuous mind

D elight they give, but outward charms decay,

  A nd like the fragrant flowers, they fade away;

A fair one love who still is well inclin'd,

  G ive her the praise who has a virtuous mind:

M ay both your hearts in mutual love unite,

  R est in true peace, and permanent delight,

A nd if your hearts unite as well as hands,

  O may you pleasure find in Hymen's bands;

N ew joys will then arise, if both agree,

  S incere and constant may you ever be:

T hus may you settle in the world with joy,

  S uperior pleasures seek, which ne'er can cloy.

ACROSTIC

On the Author's Name.

J oyless, kind Sirs, I've known my long life through,

A baleful scene of suff'rings, care, and woe;

M y folly me expos'd to guilt and shame,

E nduring hardships, bearing all the blame:

S ince in old age I've not my sins forsook,

C an I to God for pard'ning mercy look?

H ow dare I lift my guilty eyes to heav'n,

A nd e'er presume to say "my sin's forgiv'n?"

M y heart's defil'd, my soul is stain'd with sin,

B ut Christ can wash the filthy dungeon clean,

E rase my crimes, and true composure give,

R enew my heart, while I more grace receive,

S o may I ever in his name believe.

ACROSTIC ON HARVEST.

(James Chambers, Acrostic Maker.)

J oyful is harvest, while by power divine,

A zure the sky appears, bright Sol does shine;

M ost kind our great Creator does appear,

E nriching blessings crown the smiling year:

S urely we should our Maker love and fear.

C louds, with impending showers are rarely seen,

H ow calm! no storms tempestuous intervene;

A lert the farmer to the corn-fields walks,

M ildly with the industrious reapers talks,

B rings them some choice old beer, with harvest cakes;

E ach gratefully to the kind master speaks,

R eady in all respects on him to wait,

S teadfast, and faithful in a servile state.

A promise did our blest Creator make,

C are of his people he'd at all times take,

R ule o'er them hourly with a father's care;

O 'er all his works his tender mercies are:

S till, he to us, tho' we have not him serv'd,

T he appointed weeks of harvest has reserv'd,

I nclines the hearts of labourers truly wise

C hrist's precepts, and rich favours still to prize.

M ay gratitude, when harvest ends, abound,

A nd when the sparkling glass of wine goes round,

K indred and friends surround the festal board,

E nrich'd with mercy from their bounteous Lord,

R evere and praise his power with one accord.

DOUBLE ACROSTIC.

(John Pitcher, Woodbridge—Betsy Browne, Southwold).

J oy fills the mind when
O 'erspreads the hills,
H ow pleasant 'tis
N ow pleasing scenes the
P inks and sweet roses
I n gardens now
T he harvest comes,
C rops of fine corn
H ow blest the scene
E ludes dull care, I
R etire we may,
W alking in cooling
O may true love and peace
O ur minds agree in
D aily may we in
B e pleasant and quite
R eplete with joy, may
I n peace and love unite
D elight may we enjoy, and
G oodness and love, with true
E ver be joyful till this life shall cease.

B right Aurora's dawn
E lucidates the lawn;
T o walk the dewy fields,
S ummer season yields,
Y ield a rich perfume,
B right florets are in bloom,
R ich stores the country yields,
O 'erspreads the spacious fields;
W hen Betsy's charming voice,
N ow in heart rejoice,
E xpress true virtuous love,
S hades, or tufted grove;
O ur hearts unite,
U nion and delight,
T rue content abide,
H appy, void of pride;
W e, in Hymen's bands,
O ur hearts and hands,
L ive in peace,
D elight increase,

DOUBLE ACROSTIC.

(Ann Prest, Lewisham, is a Courteous Lady).

A recent verse I for a Lady write,
N or fear but 'twill S ome courteous mind delight;
N ew verdant scenes will soon A dorn the grove,
P rize blessings still C elestial, sent in love,
R etire in rural walks, O 'er fertile fields,
E ach vernal scene U nrivall'd pleasure yields;
S upernal power adore, R evere kind Heav'n,
T hat has pure joys in T ender mercy giv'n:
L ove in true breasts E xcites a flame divine,
E ach grateful views Heaven's O rb with brilliance shine,
W hile feather'd choirs U nite to cheer the grove,
I nspiring virtuous S entiments of love.
S hould e'er in mutual L ove and true delight,
H ymen's soft bands your A m'rous hearts unite,
A dorn'd with charms that D ecorate the mind,
M ay chaste endearments Y ield true joys refin'd.

DOUBLE ACROSTIC.

(Mr. Samuel Golden, a Waiter in a Shop).

M ild, pleasant, calm,   A nd bright is smiling Spring,
R eplete with joy   W ing'd choirists sweetly sing,
S erene the vernal   A ir, you pass the hours
A mongst the snow-drops, or   I n roseate bowers;
M using on pure, on   T rue supernal love,
U nite with these,   E xtol the power above,
E lude vain joys,   R ejoice in works divine
L ucid while solar rays   I n splendour shine,
G ay Ladies bright may   N ow for pleasure rove,
O ft muse on florid scenes   A nd virtuous love,
L ively bright scenes,   S oon from florets gay
D aily with rapid   H aste you're call'd away,
E ntering the shop, you   O n fair Ladies wait,
N or can you fail to   P rize your peaceful state.

TREBLE ACROSTIC.

(Robert Garnham lately married an amiable Lady):

R eview the	L adies fair, in rich	A ttire, [array,
O ur gardens all	A dorn'd with	N eat
B ridegroom and bride	T he vernal scene	A dmire
E lude dull care, while	E nters smiling	M ay,
R ich florets, Squires and	L adies fair	I nvite,
T heir thoughts, in bloom of	Y outh in praise	A scend
G reat Sol sheds forth in	M ay a lustre	B right,
A nd favors good	A nd great, kind heaven does	L end,
R eviving spring	R ich mercies does	E xtend
N ow may true joy,	R eplete with virtuous	L ove,
H ymenial blessings	I n your life	A ppear
A lert, yet true,	E xcel the faithful	- D ove,
M ay peace and praise	D elight—adorn thy	Years.

TREBLE ACROSTIC.

(I have made a Rhyme,
Not Verse sublime,
At Christmas Time).

I seldom at	N ew Christmas see	A feast,
H ear of choice cates,	O f no rich dainties	T aste,
A nd gentry who	T heir languid spirits	C heer,
V erses still deign to	V iew, of which they	H ear;
E nvy I'd fain	E lude, let it	R etire,
M ay each good wish my	R ecent theme	I nspire;
A t this auspicious	S eason, friends	S incere
D elight in joy,	E rase the orphan's	T ear.
E lusive to dire	S cenes, I'll grieve no	M ore,
A spire to things	U nseen, heaven's power	A dore,
R esign to Providence for	B lessings are in	S tore;
H eaven's favors rich	L ife's fading joys	T ranscend,
Y et trying scenes	I ntrude, dull cares	I mpend:
M ay I once more indulge	M y virent	M use,
E motions it	E xcites, kind friends	E xcuse.

TREBLE ACROSTIC.

(Young Ladies play on the Piano Forte at Christmas Time).

Y oung Ladies walk	O 'er fields for vernal	A ir,
O r talk with kindred	N ear, or lover	T rue;
U niting thus	T o chace away dull	C are,
N ew flowers appear, and	H erbs in lovely	H ue:
G entry those herbs	E steem when Spring shall	R ise,
L ilies most fair with	P urest white	I ncrease,
A nd radiant light	I llumes the azure	S kies:
D elight will then	A ttend those steps to	T race,
I f Christmas please	N ot like to smiling	M ay,
E namell'd fields spread	O 'er with rich	A ttire,
S uperbly dress'd	F air Ladies blithsome	S tray:
		[lyre,
P lay on Piano Forte	O r strike the	T uneful
L adies sweet strains	R epeat, the ear	I nvite,
A ccents most sacred, hail	T he God of	M ight,
Y ield solace, and	E xtatic joys	E xcite.

TREBLE ACROSTIC.

(Acrostic for Robert Roe, Printer in Copperplate, and Engraver, Cambridge).

A dorn'd superb,	P ellucid rays	A ppear,
C reation shines	R efulgent, far and	N ear,
R esplendent scenes	I n Autumn yield	D elight,
O mnifick power may	N ew applause	E xcite;
S pring will revive,	T he grand parterre look	N eat,
T hose florid scenes will	E ntertain the	G reat;
I n Spring the blushing	R ose sheds beauties	R are,
C arnations breathe perfume	I n vernal	A ir;
F rail man must sure, when	N ature's works he's	V iew'd,
O bey celestial	C alls, each vice	E lude,
R esent all thoughts	O bscene, and converse	R ude;
R ich gentry, void of	P ride, dear babes	Caress,'
O bedient children	P rize, of meek	A ddress,
B lessings attend, no	E nemies	M olest;
E namell'd scenes	R evive the languid	B reast:
R ich neat engravings	P olish'd, and	R efin'd,
T o please true friends to	L ove who are	I nclin'd,
R elations at his	A bsence seem	Distrest,
O ld Ipswich friends will	T reat a welcome	G uest,
E ach hour on Christmas	E ve much joy will be	E xprest.

TREBLE ACROSTIC.

(James Chambers, Itinerent Poet, despised by Man).

J oy sometimes visits one	**I** n sordid	**D** ress,
A nd he does cordial	**T** hanks to heaven	**E** xpress.
M ost cruel foes	**I** nfest to filch his	**S** tore,
E late with pride they	**N** ew contempt will	**P** our;
S arcastic speech vain tongues	**E** mit	**I** ndeed;
C omfort, and peace of mind	**R** etire with	**S** peed.
H ere I, who powers	**E** xert in verse t'	**E** xcel,
A m oft advis'd	**N** ear Cambridge town to	**D** well;
M ay worthy Gentry	**T** here a cottage	**B** uild
B y limpid streams, 'twill	**P** eace, and solace	**Y** ield;
E rected on the verge	**O** f Soham bright	**M** ere,
R esiding there,	**E** ach prospect will	**A** ppear
S till brighter, if	**T** rue christian friends live	**N** ear.

FINIS.